Good Practice Guide: **Adjudication**

RIBA Good Practice Guides

Other titles in this series:

Good Practice Guide:
Adjudication

Mair Coombes Davies

RIBA Publishing

© Mair Coombes Davies, 2011

Published by RIBA Publishing, 15 Bonhill Street, London EC2P 2EA

ISBN 978 1 85946 395 6

Stock code 74618

British Library Cataloguing-in-Publication Data
A catalogue record for this book is available from the British Library.

Commissioning Editor: James Thompson
Project Editor: Alasdair Deas
Designed by: Ben Millbank
Typeset by: Academic + Technical, Bristol
Printed and bound by Polestar Wheatons

RIBA Publishing is part of RIBA Enterprises Ltd.

www.ribaenterprises.com

Author's dedication

To Taliesin

Series foreword

The *Good Practice Guide* series has been specifically developed to provide architects, and other construction professionals, with practical advice and guidance on a range of topics that affect them, and the management of their business, on a day-to-day basis.

All of the guides in the series are written in an easy-to-read, straightforward style. The guides are not meant to be definitive texts on the particular subject in question, but each guide will be the reader's first point of reference, offering them a quick overview of the key points and then provide them with a 'route map' for finding further, more detailed information. Where appropriate, check-lists, tables, diagrams, and case studies will be included to aid ease-of-use.

Good Practice Guide: Adjudication

Adjudication is the predominant means of resolving disputes in architecture and the construction industry. It allows projects to be completed without wasting time and cost in litigation, and is prescribed by statute as the default means of resolving a dispute whenever a construction contract is in place.

While adjudication may be swift and cost-effective when compared to other methods of dispute resolution, it goes without saying that the most effective way of saving time and money is to avoid the dispute in the first place. There is a wealth of guidance available that can help you do just that – both in the RIBA *Good Practice Guides* and other RIBA publications, such as the *Architect's Job Book* and *Handbook of Practice Management* – all of which will help you minimise risk and ensure the best project outcomes.

But if a dispute does arise, then this short, clear guide will make an invaluable first stopping-point in the adjudication process. It explains the background to adjudication and compares it in a balanced and informative way against the other available dispute resolution methods, before going on to explain what you should expect to happen and what you need to do throughout the process.

Angela Brady, *President, RIBA*

About the author

Dr Mair Coombes Davies BSc BArch PhD RIBA FCIArb is Chair of the RIBA President's Advisory Committee on Dispute Resolution.

She is dual qualified as an architect and a barrister, receiving degrees from the University of Wales, including a PhD in law.

She has conducted over a thousand separate adjudications, arbitrations and mediations and is a member of several adjudication, arbitration and mediation panels, including those of the RIBA.

She has lectured widely on alternative dispute resolution and is responsible for books and articles on this subject. She is editor of *The Guidance*, the Chartered Institute of Arbitrators' code of ethical practice, procedure and performance for qualified adjudicators, arbitrators and mediators around the world. She has led and sat on specialist committees on the development and future of dispute resolution for the RIBA, the Chartered Institute of Arbitrators and the General Council of the Bar. She represents the RIBA at the Architects' Council of Europe Working Party on Dispute Resolution, Brussels.

Acknowledgements

I would like to thank all those who have been a help and inspiration to me not only in the good practice of arbitration and adjudication but also in writing this guide. In particular Adam Williamson, the Head of Professional Standards at the RIBA, John Reilly and Ian Salisbury, both of the RIBA President's Advisory Committee on Dispute Resolution, and James Thompson, Commissioning Editor at RIBA Publishing.

Mair Coombes Davies

November 2011

Contents

Section 1
Choosing the best method to resolve a dispute

In this Section:

- *Introduction – getting the contract right*
- *Do I need to explain the dispute resolution clauses to the client?*
- *What ways are there to resolve a dispute?*
- *Choices: adjudication and arbitration*
- *Drawbacks of adjudication and arbitration*
- *When to choose adjudication*
- *When to choose arbitration*
- *Good practice summary*

Introduction – getting the contract right

It is a fact of life that disputes arise. It is also a fact of life that there are many ways to resolve disputes.

Adjudication is one way of resolving a dispute in a construction contract.

The different ways of resolving disputes can be confusing in their variety and the complexity of their procedures. The importance of dispute *avoidance* is that it cuts through this confusion. It means that a practice does not have to divert time, effort and money away from its core business. The best method of dispute avoidance is also the most simple and the most frequently overlooked: *make sure you get the contract right.*

1

Getting the contract right in the first place is crucial. If a contract is right then it may help in reducing costly and time-consuming disputes as well as helping to ensure that a project is completed on time and on budget.

There are at least three things which should be done and three things which should not be done to get a contract right.

The three things which should be done are:

- Make sure there is a complete, auditable paper trail, although it is possible to go to adjudication on the basis of an oral contract.
- Where a contract is made up of a number of documents, make sure that each document is consistent within itself and consistent with all other documents. For example, in a typical contract between an architect and a client based on the *RIBA Standard Agreement 2010*, there may be six or more contract documents for the appointment of the architect, including the *Conditions of Appointment*, the *Schedules of Project Data, Services and Fees and Expenses*, *Memorandum of Agreement* or *Letter of Appointment*; whereas in a JCT building contract the contract documents may include the agreement, conditions, contract drawings, priced documents or specification, invitations to tender and tenders to and by named subcontractors.
- Make sure the terms of the contract are expressed in plain, easily understood language so that they cannot be misinterpreted.

The three things which should not be done are:

- Having no record or an incomplete record of the terms and conditions of a contract (a frequent problem with oral contracts that leads to many disputes).
- Stating within a contract that the terms of a previous contract are to apply without having first carefully checked that they are appropriate. For example, the first contract might have required insurance cover of a certain amount, but if the second contract is of higher value the insurance cover is likely to be inadequate.
- Forgetting to ensure that the contractor actually gives the client a document which the contractor is required to give under the contract, e.g. a bond or insurance.

Do I need to explain the dispute resolution clauses to the client?

In a word, 'Yes'.

But, the degree of explanation depends on who the client is. If the client is very experienced and has access to legal advice then the explanation may not be as detailed as that given to a client who has had no experience of architecture, procurement and construction and is not advised by a lawyer.

The key point to remember is, quite simply, that it is good practice to highlight the dispute resolution clauses in any contract to all clients. The adjudication clauses, as well as any arbitration, mediation and litigation clauses, should be clearly explained to and understood by the client.

It is worth spending time with the client going through the implications of the dispute resolution clauses so that the client is completely comfortable with them. If you do not, then later it is quite possible for the client to say you took advantage of their lack of experience by merely providing documentation without explanation, knowing the client did not have independent advice. In other words, the dispute resolution clauses are unfair terms. So, to show that the negotiations were carried out in good faith, make sure you:

- read through the terms of the contract with the client
- clearly and simply explain the implications of the dispute resolution clauses
- recommend the client obtains independent legal advice if the client is not already advised by a lawyer
- leave the draft contract with the client for the client to consider at their leisure
- agree each clause separately
- make a detailed note of the negotiations with the client
- provide the client with a record of your negotiations – this can be done by way of the Letter of Appointment enclosing the agreed contract for the signature of the client, and
- mention in the Letter of Appointment, 'If there is anything you do not understand please do not hesitate to contact and discuss it with me'.

A very useful small booklet to have as an aide-memoire is Roland Phillips' *A Short Guide to Consumer Rights in Construction Contracts* (RIBA Publishing, 2010).

KEY POINT: *Draw the attention of the client to any adjudication and other dispute resolution clauses in the contract.*

What ways are there to resolve a dispute?

Where problems are encountered within a contract which lead to a dispute between the parties then, depending on the terms of the contract, there may be a number of ways in which the dispute can be resolved. Adjudication is one of the most frequently used forms of dispute resolution in architecture and the construction industry. Other ways to resolve disputes include arbitration, conciliation, dispute resolution boards, early neutral evaluation, expert determination, litigation, mediation, med/arb and negotiation. The differences between them are described in Table 1.1.

Choices: adjudication and arbitration

If you wish to refer a dispute for resolution then in a number of standard forms of contracts you are given a choice between arbitration and adjudication. For example, the RIBA *Standard Conditions of Appointment for an Architect* contains adjudication, arbitration and litigation options:

> **Part A. A9 Dispute resolution**
> *A9.1 Any dispute or difference arising out of this Agreement may be referred to adjudication, legal proceedings or arbitration by the Client or the Architect in accordance with the provisions of this Agreement...*

There are significant differences between adjudication and arbitration. They include those which are set out in Table 1.2.

Drawbacks of adjudication and arbitration

Adjudication and arbitration do have some drawbacks, for example:

* an adjudicator's decision is likely to be enforced by the courts provided that the adjudicator has answered the correct question, even if that decision contained obvious errors or was wrong in fact or law
* in arbitration the right of a party to appeal is limited. Appealing to the court against an arbitrator's award is restricted to challenging the award on the grounds of a serious irregularity or on a point of law. The leave of the court first has to be obtained if the parties do not agree to the proceedings.

When to choose adjudication

The reasons for choosing adjudication include the following considerations:

- a quick decision is needed, that is, within 28 days of referral, extended by up to 14 days with the consent of the referring party (i.e. the party by whom the dispute was referred) or such longer period as is agreed by the parties after the dispute has been referred
- tight cost control is required – as the whole process should be completed very quickly there is only so much that can be done within such a limited period
- there is a construction contract
- an adjudicator from within the industry is needed, who will have the knowledge, experience and industry wisdom to get to the heart of the dispute quickly
- the parties recognise that the speed with which a decision is reached might lead to an element of rough justice
- a final resolution of the dispute is not needed. An adjudicator's decision is temporary. It is only binding until the dispute is finally determined by agreement, legal proceedings or arbitration.

When to choose arbitration

As a quick guide, the reasons for choosing arbitration, either initially, instead of adjudication, or to decide a dispute afresh after it has not been resolved at adjudication, include the following:

- privacy and confidentiality are needed
- the dispute is specialised in nature
- a resolution of the dispute is required without delay and unnecessary cost
- there is an arbitration agreement in writing between the parties
- the parties wish to appoint their own arbitrator, who has a particular expertise that is suitable for resolving their dispute
- the parties have agreed the institute or professional body that is going to appoint the arbitrator
- a flexible procedure is needed which can be tailored to the dispute to make the best use of the time and the location of the parties, leading to greater convenience and tighter cost control.

If you choose arbitration then the other party may have no option but to accept that choice. Conversely, if you are the respondent in the dispute and the claimant chooses arbitration then you must continue with the arbitration (unless you have not taken a 'step in the action', in which case you can apply for the dispute to be heard by the court).

TABLE 1.1: *Different methods of dispute resolution*

Dispute resolution	Process	Speed of process	Costs	Procedure
Adjudication	Private	Quick 28 days, can be extended by up to 14 days with referring party consent or longer period if both parties agree.	Moderate The adjudicator may determine and apportion between the parties the adjudicator's fees.	Statutory formality The adjudicator decides the procedure to be followed.
Arbitration	Private	Quick to moderate	Moderate Parties pay the arbitrator. The arbitrator may make an award allocating the costs of the arbitration between the parties subject to any agreement of the parties.	Formal but flexible
Conciliation	Private	Quick Usually lasts between half a day and two days, with most lasting one day.	Low to moderate Fees of the conciliator shared equally by the parties.	Informal
Dispute resolution board (DRB)	Private	DRB lasts the life of a building contract. A recommendation can be made quickly by the DRB once it has been notified of a dispute.	Moderate Fees of the DRB are shared equally by the parties.	Informal
Early neutral evaluation	Private	Quick	Low Fees of evaluator shared equally by the parties.	Informal
Expert determination	Private	Quick	Low The contract may give the expert power to direct a party to pay costs.	Informal

Method	Result
Statutory procedure by which any party to a construction contract, with some exceptions, has a right to have a dispute decided by an adjudicator. The referring party serves a Notice of Adjudication on the responding party, applies to a nominating body (ANB) for an adjudicator to be nominated if no adjudicator is named in the contract, then serves the Referral on the other party and the adjudicator giving particulars of the dispute, a summary of contentions relied on, a statement of the relief or remedy sought and documents relied on. The responding party serves a written statement of contentions on which it relies together with any material it wishes the adjudicator to consider. Adjudicator takes the initiative in ascertaining the facts and the law necessary to determine the dispute. The adjudicator must reach a decision within 28 days or any extended date.	The decision is temporary until the dispute is resolved by litigation, arbitration or agreement.
Arbitration is governed by the Arbitration Act 1996 and any rules referred to in any contract or agreement between the parties. The dispute or disagreement will be resolved by the award of the arbitrator (who is a neutral, independent third party) in accordance with the relevant law and rules. The procedure of an arbitration can be developed to that which is most suitable for the parties' dispute, e.g. a documents only arbitration, an arbitration with a hearing, or giving inquisitorial powers to the arbitrator.	Award is binding. An award can be enforced upon application to the court in the same manner as a judgment or order of the court. Limited right to appeal.
As for mediation, except that the conciliator can also suggest a solution which may be given orally or in writing.	Non binding unless parties consent.
DRB of three neutral, professional members, e.g. architect, engineer or quantity surveyor, is appointed before construction (one selected by the client, approved by the contractor; one selected by the contractor, approved by the client; one selected by the two DRB members, approved by the parties). DRB members select one of them as chair, approved by the client and the contractor. DRB is given contract documents and regular construction information and makes site visits. A dispute is referred by a party to the DRB, which reviews it, considers the contract documentation, correspondence etc., holds an informal hearing and makes a written recommendation for resolving the dispute.	Recommendation is not binding.
Neutral third party expert, usually a lawyer, gives an opinion on the chances of success for each party if they were to pursue litigation.	Opinion is not binding.
Parties jointly appoint an independent expert to determine a dispute through his or her own expertise and investigations.	Parties decide whether or not the decision is binding.

TABLE 1.1: *Continued*

Dispute resolution	Process	Speed of process	Costs	Procedure
Litigation	Public (normally)	Moderate to slow	Moderate to high Court fees are paid by the parties. The court has a discretion as to whether costs are payable by one party to another, the amount of those costs and when they are to be paid. The general rule is that the unsuccessful party will be ordered to pay the costs of the successful party, but the court may make a different order.	Formal
Mediation	Private	Quick Usually a mediation lasts between half a day and two days, with most lasting one day.	Low to moderate Fees of the mediator shared equally by the parties.	Informal
Med/Arb	Private	Moderate See *mediation* and *arbitration*.	Moderate See *mediation* and *arbitration*.	See *mediation* and *arbitration*.
Negotiation	Private	Quick to slow	Low to moderate Parties pay their own costs unless otherwise agreed.	Informal

Method	Result
Court legal proceedings to resolve a dispute. Generally the procedure is as follows. Pre-action protocols encourage the frank and early exchange of information about a prospective claim and any defence to it to enable parties to avoid litigation by agreeing a settlement of a claim before the commencement of proceedings, or to support the efficient management of proceedings where litigation cannot be avoided. An action begins when a *Claim Form* filed by the claimant is issued by the court. The claimant also files *Particulars of Claim* containing a concise statement of the nature of the claim and specifying the remedy sought. The Claim Form and Particulars of Claim are served on the defendant within a time limit. The defendant files an *Acknowledgement of Service* and has a time limit within which to serve a *Defence* (and *Counterclaim* if appropriate, for damages or other relief against the claimant) stating: which of the allegations are denied, giving reasons and the defendant's version of events; which allegations the defendant is unable to admit or deny but requires the claimant to prove; and which allegations the defendant admits. The claimant may serve a *Reply* to the Defence if the claimant wishes to allege facts in answer to the Defence which were not included in the Particulars of Claim, and defend any allegations made in any Counterclaim. A case management conference is held by a judge at the outset and then throughout the proceedings to ensure that the real issues are identified, a realistic timetable is ordered for the resolution of the action and costs are controlled. *Directions* can include allocation of the case to fast- or multi-track procedures, disclosure and inspection of documents, exchange of witness statements, expert evidence, fixing dates for a pre-trial review and the trial itself, the preparation by the claimant of an indexed and paginated trial bundle of documents (for use of the court and parties) and the service by both parties of skeleton arguments and chronologies. At the trial each party presents its evidence and witnesses for examination in chief, cross-examination and re-examination by the other party, Generally, the claimant has the burden of proof, i.e. the claimant must produce enough evidence to persuade the judge on the balance of probability that the claim should succeed (on some matters the defendant may have the burden of proof). Following the evidence, the defendant then the claimant make closing submissions and the judge gives judgment.	Judgment is final and binding subject to a right to appeal.
Parties may provide the mediator with a succinct written summary of the dispute. At a joint meeting the parties make verbal presentations, followed by private sessions between the mediator and each party (also joint sessions) where the mediator assists parties in reaching agreement.	Non binding unless parties consent to settlement.
Parties attempt to settle the dispute through mediation. If a settlement is not reached then the mediator acting as arbitrator resolves the dispute by arbitration.	See *mediation* and *arbitration*.
The parties try to reach an agreement by discussion.	Non binding unless parties consent to settlement.

TABLE 1.2: *Some differences between adjudication and arbitration*

Item	Adjudication	Arbitration
Act	Housing Grants, Construction and Regeneration Act 1996, Part 2 (as amended)	Arbitration Act 1996
Agreement	Must have a construction contract. It can be either in writing, oral or partly oral and partly in writing	Arbitration agreement evidenced in writing
Timetable	28 days; extended by up to 14 days with consent of the referring party, or a longer period if both parties agree	Arbitrator decides subject to the parties' right to agree any matter
Procedure	Adjudicator may take the initiative in ascertaining the facts and the law necessary to determine the dispute and decides the procedure to be followed	Arbitrator decides all procedural and evidential matters subject to the parties' right to agree any matter
Result	Decision is binding only until the dispute is finally resolved by legal proceedings, arbitration or parties' agreement	Award is final and binding on parties and persons claiming through or under them
Appeal	No statutory mechanism for appeal; dispute heard afresh in legal proceedings or arbitration	Appeal to the court only on a question of law, with the agreement of all parties or with the leave of the court
Enforcement	Litigation or arbitration	An award may, by leave of the court, be enforced in the same manner as a judgment or order of the court

Although the parties are free to agree on the number of arbitrators to form the tribunal, usually the arbitral tribunal will consist of a sole arbitrator. An arbitrator is an independent, impartial third party. Generally, an arbitrator is professionally qualified with an industry background or specialist technical expertise suitable for the subject in dispute. For example, in a dispute between an architect and a client where the architect claims fees for architectural services, the arbitrator may be dual qualified as an architect and lawyer. The arbitrator will make a judgment on the dispute which will be set out in an award. The award is binding upon the parties when it is issued. It may, by leave of the court, be enforced in the same manner as a judgment or order of the court.

GOOD PRACTICE SUMMARY

- Draw the attention of the client to any adjudication and other dispute resolution clauses in the contract.
- Clearly explain the adjudication clauses to the client as well as the arbitration, mediation and litigation clauses.
- Make sure that the client understands the implications of each dispute resolution clause and agrees to each of them.
- Leave a copy of the contract with the client, suggest the client reads it through and obtains legal advice.
- Make sure you send the client a Letter of Appointment recording the negotiations, stating what has been agreed on each dispute resolution clause and enclosing the agreed contract for signature.

Section 2
The adjudication agreement

In this Section:

- *Introduction*
- *The right to adjudication*
- *Inclusions and exclusions*
- *How much of an adjudication agreement must be in writing?*
- *What does 'in writing' mean?*
- *Your role is important*
- *Good practice summary*

Introduction

The first question in any adjudication is often, 'Is there an adjudication agreement?'.

Such a straightforward question can be the start of intense work over a very short period of time, so it pays to be prepared.

The right to adjudication

Adjudication is the right of a party to a construction contract to have a dispute determined by an adjudicator at any time. A construction contract is quite simply an agreement for the carrying out of construction operations.[1]

---

[1] See the Housing Grants, Construction and Regeneration Act 1996, Part 2 (as amended), sections 104–105 for an exact, statutory definition of a construction contract.

The 'right' to adjudication is provided by the Housing Grants, Construction and Regeneration Act 1996, Part 2 (as amended).[2] The standard forms of contract, such as the RIBA and JCT forms, all cover adjudication. If a construction contract does not make provision for one or more of the various terms relating to adjudication required by the Act then terms will be implied into the contract so that a default scheme will apply, called the *Scheme for Construction Contracts*. The Scheme applies not only to written construction contracts, but also to oral construction contracts or those which are partly oral and partly in writing. Oral contracts are, by their very nature, considerably less detailed than, say, a standard RIBA or JCT contract, so it is quite likely that the Scheme will be used far more in situations where there is an oral agreement (or one that is mostly oral) than where a written agreement is in place. It is therefore good practice to be familiar with the Scheme.[3] The Scheme differs slightly depending on whether the construction contract is for construction operations in England, Wales, Scotland or Northern Ireland.[4]

KEY POINT: Be familiar with the Scheme for Construction Contracts.

Inclusions and exclusions

Adjudication could affect most construction contracts, whether in writing, oral or partly written and partly oral. This includes contracts for architectural design, surveying or advice on building, engineering and landscape, as well as the construction, alteration, repair, maintenance, extension, decoration or demolition

---

[2] Housing Grants, Construction and Regeneration Act 1996, Part 2 (as amended), section 108. The 1996 Act was amended by the Local Democracy, Economic Development and Construction Act 2009. See Appendix 1.

[3] See Appendix 2.

[4] The different Scheme regulations are:
- In England, the Scheme for Construction Contracts (England and Wales) Regulations 1998 (Amendment) (England) Regulations 2011.
- In Wales, the Scheme for Construction Contracts (England and Wales) Regulations 1998 (Amendment) (Wales) Regulations 2011 (Scheme for Construction Contracts (Wales) Regulations 2011).
- In Scotland, the Scheme for Construction Contracts (Scotland) Amendment Regulations 2011 (Scheme for Construction Contracts (Scotland) Regulations 2011).
- In Northern Ireland, the Construction Contracts (Amendment) Act (Northern Ireland) 2011.

of buildings, preparatory work such as site clearance, earth-moving and excavation, and the installation of fittings such as heating, lighting, drainage and sanitation systems. Make sure you check the date of the construction contract against the commencement date of the Act (as amended) to ensure that an oral construction contract, or one that is partly oral and partly in writing, is caught by its provisions.

Adjudication is excluded from some construction contracts. For example, the Act (as amended) does not apply to purely artistic work. It also does not apply to a construction contract with a residential occupier,[5] in other words a construction contract which *principally* relates to operations on a dwelling that one of the parties to the contract occupies, or intends to occupy, as their residence. It is worth bearing in mind that the conversion of, for example, a barn to a dwelling is still a residential occupier contract even though occupation is not possible until after completion. While, under the Act (as amended), there is no right to go to adjudication with a residential occupier, nonetheless the contract (for example, the RIBA standard forms) itself may provide for adjudication, in which case the right to go to adjudication arises under the contract.

KEY POINT: Make sure there is a complete, auditable paper trail, even though you can go to adjudication on the basis of an oral contract.

How much of an adjudication agreement must be in writing?

Since the amendment of the Act, an adjudication agreement does *not* have to be in writing.[6] Nevertheless, it is still good practice to ensure that all the terms of the contract are in writing, not least because this ensures that there is an auditable paper trail should things go wrong, but also because the Act (as amended) still requires the contract to include *some* provisions in writing. Those provisions are to:[7]

---

[5] Housing Grants, Construction and Regeneration Act 1996, Part 2 (as amended), section 106.
[6] Housing Grants, Construction and Regeneration Act 1996, Part 2, section 107's provisions, applicable only to agreements in writing, were deleted by the Local Democracy, Economic Development and Construction Act 2009.
[7] Housing Grants, Construction and Regeneration Act 1996, Part 2 (as amended), section 108(2).

- enable a party to give notice at any time of an intention to refer a dispute to adjudication
- provide a timetable with the object of securing the appointment of the adjudicator and referral of the dispute to the adjudicator within seven days of such notice
- require the adjudicator to reach a decision within 28 days of referral or such longer period as is agreed by the parties after the dispute has been referred
- allow the adjudicator to extend the period of 28 days by up to 14 days, with the consent of the party by whom the dispute was referred (that is, the referring party)
- impose a duty on the adjudicator to act impartially
- enable the adjudicator to take the initiative in ascertaining the facts and the law.

Other provisions which must be in writing are to:

- provide that the decision of the adjudicator is binding until the dispute is finally determined by legal proceedings, by arbitration (if the contract provides for arbitration or the parties otherwise agree to arbitration) or by agreement[8]
- permit the adjudicator to correct the decision so as to remove a clerical or typographical error arising by accident or omission[9]
- provide that the adjudicator is not liable for anything done or omitted in the discharge or purported discharge of the adjudicator's functions unless the act or omission is in bad faith, and that any employee or agent of the adjudicator is similarly protected from liability.[10]

From a practical point of view it is important that you check all the contract documents (if it is a written contract) or your records (if it is an oral contract) to make sure that the adjudication provisions are included and are consistent. The reason is that, if the contract does not contain these provisions in writing then the adjudication provisions of the Scheme for Construction Contracts apply. If the contract does contain them then the parties can either devise their own rules or (more usually) include in the contract a reference to a set of

---

[8] Housing Grants, Construction and Regeneration Act 1996, Part 2 (as amended), section 108(3).
[9] Housing Grants, Construction and Regeneration Act 1996, Part 2 (as amended), section 108(3A).
[10] Housing Grants, Construction and Regeneration Act 1996, Part 2 (as amended), section 108(4).

adjudication rules, for example, the *Construction Industry Council Model Adjudication Procedure*. Frequently, even when the contract contains the minimum provisions, it will refer to and incorporate the Scheme for Construction Contracts.

KEY POINT: Check that all the contract documents have consistent adjudication clauses.

What does 'in writing' mean?

The meaning of the words 'in writing' can be very wide. It not only means a document headed Contract or Adjudication Agreement which has been signed by the parties, it may cover any means by which a construction contract and the adjudication provisions within it are recorded. For example:

* agreements made in writing, whether or not signed
* agreements made by exchange of written communications
* agreements which are 'evidenced in writing'
* agreements which are not actually in writing but which are recorded by one of the parties, or by a third party, with the authority of the parties to the agreement
* exchanges of written submissions in adjudication, arbitration or legal proceedings in which the existence of a construction contract otherwise than in writing is alleged by one party and not denied by the other.

Your role is important

It is crucially important to check that an adjudication agreement is correct.

If you are using one of the standard forms of appointment or building contracts then they will cover the requirements of the Act (as amended). However, make sure that any amendments do not go against its requirements, and that any references to adjudication are consistent within a document or across a series of documents making up the contract. The bullet points above provide a helpful checklist. Making these checks should not take long and could save you time and money in future.

┌─────────────────── **GOOD PRACTICE SUMMARY** ───────────────────┐

• Be familiar with the Scheme for Construction Contracts.
• Make sure there is a complete, auditable paper trail, even though you can go to adjudication on an oral contract.
• Check that all the contract documents have consistent adjudication clauses.

└──┘

Section 3
Starting adjudication: made easy

In this Section:

- *Introduction*
- *The whole process*
- *Is there a dispute?*
- *What should a Notice of Adjudication contain?*
- *What to do upon receipt of a Notice of Adjudication*
- *Nominating an adjudicator*
- *How is an adjudicator nominated by an ANB?*
- *What happens when the adjudicator is nominated?*
- *Good practice summary*

Introduction

The key points of adjudication are its speed and efficiency.

It is important to act quickly and respond quickly as adjudication is such a fast procedure. Preparation beforehand and tight organisation during adjudication will help to ensure smooth progress.

The whole process

Adjudication is a logical progression from the issue of the Notice of Adjudication to the Decision of the adjudicator. The overall process is similar in any adjudication:

1. A Notice of Intention to Refer a Dispute to Adjudication (usually called a *Notice of Adjudication*) is given by the referring party to the responding party and, if

FIGURE 3.1: *The adjudication procedure*

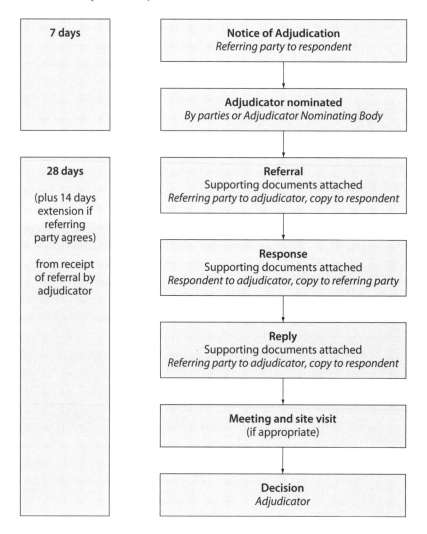

appropriate, to the Adjudicator Nominating Body (ANB) – the object is to secure both the nomination of the adjudicator and the referral of the dispute to the adjudicator within seven days of the giving of the *Notice of Adjudication.*

2. Nomination of the adjudicator either by the parties or by an ANB, such as the RIBA, the Construction Industry Council, the Royal Institution of Chartered Surveyors (RICS) or the Chartered Institute of Arbitrators (see *How is an adjudicator nominated by an ANB?* below).

3. The *Referral* is sent by the referring party to the responding party and the adjudicator.

4. A *Response to the Referral* is given by the responding party if the adjudicator gives a direction to do so.

5. A *Reply* is given by the referring party if so directed by the adjudicator.

6. A *Decision* by the adjudicator is given within 28 days of the adjudicator receiving the *Referral* or such longer period as is agreed by the parties after the dispute has been referred. The adjudicator is allowed to extend the 28-day period by up to 14 days, with the consent of the referring party.

Is there a dispute?

How do you, as the referring party, determine that you can accurately call a problem a dispute? This is a grey area but it is of practical significance. The problem must have crystallised into a dispute before you write your Notice of Adjudication. If it has not, then any Notice of Adjudication is invalid and the adjudicator will have no jurisdiction.

Some pointers on establishing whether a dispute has crystallised:

- Before starting adjudication, write to the other party setting out what the problem is, summarising the background to the problem, what you claim and a date by which you would like a reply. The time for a response should be realistic. So if your claim is straightforward, then a reply in 7 to 14 days could be reasonable. On the other hand, if it is complex, then several weeks or 28 days may be more appropriate.
- Take care how you word your claim because it could, at a later date, form the grounds for the Notice of Referral. If the grounds in the Notice of Referral are quite different then no dispute will have arisen and even if you achieve an adjudicator's decision in your favour, you could find that its enforcement will be refused by the court.
- A dispute will have crystallised if after discussion and negotiation your claim is rejected. A dispute will also crystallise if your claim is ignored; eight weeks is regarded as sufficient time for a claim which is ignored to become a dispute or difference,[11] although a month is more usual.[12] Indeed, even two and a

---

[11] *Cowlin Construction Ltd v. CFW Architects* [2003] EWHC 60.
[12] *Orange EBS Ltd v. ABB Ltd* [2003] EQHC 1187.

half weeks could be sufficient time; in one case an application for a stay of adjudication on the basis of no dispute was refused because the applicant had had two and a half weeks prior to the Notice of Referral to respond.[13]

KEY POINT: Make sure that a dispute has crystallised.

What should a Notice of Adjudication contain?

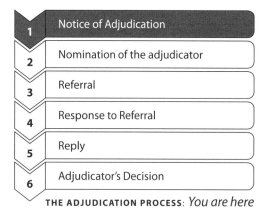

THE ADJUDICATION PROCESS: *You are here*

1. Notice of Adjudication
2. Nomination of the adjudicator
3. Referral
4. Response to Referral
5. Reply
6. Adjudicator's Decision

A Notice of Adjudication is defined as a written notice given by the referring party to another party to the contract (the responding party) of an intention to refer a dispute or difference arising under the contract to adjudication.

If your Notice of Adjudication is missing an essential piece of information, you are likely to waste time later in arguments over the validity of the notice. Prepare the notice carefully and check that it briefly sets out:

- the nature and a description of the dispute, and ensure that the grounds of the dispute have been specifically raised with the responding party beforehand so that they know what they are and have had an opportunity to address them
- details of where and when the dispute has arisen
- the nature of the redress which is sought, in other words what it is that the adjudicator is required to decide – include a breakdown showing how any time or money has been calculated
- the names and addresses of the parties to the contract who are involved in the dispute, including, where appropriate, the addresses which the parties have specified for the giving of notices.

You should send the Notice of Adjudication to the responding party. As the purpose of the Notice of Adjudication is to secure both the nomination of the

---

[13] *Beck Peppiat Ltd v. Norwest Holst Construction Ltd* [2003] EWCH 822.

adjudicator and the referral of the dispute to the adjudicator within seven days, usually (if the contract states that the appointment of the adjudicator is to be by an ANB) the notice is sent to the ANB simultaneously.

*See also:
Notice of
Adjudication,
page 49*

KEY POINT: Prepare the Notice of Adjudication carefully.

What to do upon receipt of a Notice of Adjudication

The most important thing to do when you receive a Notice of Adjudication is to respond quickly; time is short in adjudication. Remember that the object is to secure both the nomination of the adjudicator and the referral of the dispute to the adjudicator within seven days of the giving of the Notice of Adjudication.

It is vital to take the following steps:

* Immediately inform your professional indemnity insurers that you have received a Notice of Adjudication. They will need copies of all relevant documents that you have. They will discuss the situation with you and advise you on the most appropriate course to follow. They may recommend, or insist upon, the appointment of a lawyer to protect your interests.
* Check that a dispute has crystallised. At the risk of sounding repetitive, it is always worth checking if there is a viable dispute. A simple check could save you money and time.

You should also consider the following points:

* Can you do it yourself? It is perfectly possible to represent yourself in adjudication, but do not make this choice lightly. You will need to have the resources, time, finance and confidence to do so. Do not underestimate the challenge. Adjudication can be very demanding, particularly if you are working alone and are unfamiliar with the procedures and documents that must be produced. Sometimes, the choice will not be yours to make. Your professional indemnity insurer may insist that their appointed lawyer is used to represent you.
* Can you stall legitimately? Many respondents do try to delay the process by maintaining that a dispute has not crystallised and writing a very robust reply to the Notice of Adjudication.

KEY POINT: Respond quickly.

Nominating an adjudicator

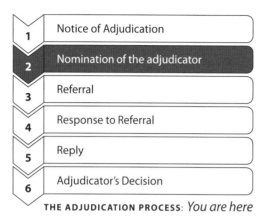

1. Notice of Adjudication
2. Nomination of the adjudicator
3. Referral
4. Response to Referral
5. Reply
6. Adjudicator's Decision

THE ADJUDICATION PROCESS: *You are here*

There are three ways in which an adjudicator can be nominated.

- *Named in the contract* – where the adjudicator is named in the construction contract, then, as the referring party, you need to include in the Notice of Adjudication served on the responding party a notice requiring them to submit the dispute to the named adjudicator.

- *Party appointment* – where the adjudicator is to be appointed by the parties then you, as the referring party, need to include in the Notice of Adjudication served on the responding party a notice requiring them to agree to the appointment of an adjudicator in respect of the dispute. You can find an adjudicator by:
  - asking a professional institution (such as the RIBA, RICS or the Chartered Institute of Adjudicators) which has a database of members who are adjudicators for the names of, say, three adjudicators who are appropriately qualified to determine your particular type of dispute
  - personal recommendation and word of mouth
  - typing, 'adjudicator', into an internet search engine.

  A joint letter from the parties should then be written to the adjudicator indicating that:
  - a dispute has arisen out of or in connection with a construction contract (if the construction contract is in writing then give its date, name and edition together with the clause number of the adjudication agreement and attach a copy of the relevant terms of the contract; if the contract is oral or partly oral and partly in writing then summarise the terms of the contract, the date when it was made, who made it and, if possible, provide a copy of any document supporting the existence of the contract)
  - the parties, named, wish to have the dispute determined by adjudication
  - the parties therefore wish to nominate *X* as adjudicator in respect of such dispute.

- *Appointment via an ANB* – an ANB is an Adjudicator Nominating Body which is entirely independent of the parties and the dispute. This is the most commonly used means of nominating an adjudicator and so is explained in more detail.

Deciding which type of nomination procedure to follow depends on the precise terms of the contract.

• If the name of the adjudicator has been included in the contract or, in the case of an oral contract, agreed before the dispute has arisen, then the nomination procedure to follow is the first one: *Named in the contract*.
• If the adjudicator is not named in the contract and if the parties are not concerned that the adjudicator has been proposed by someone who has a fundamental interest in the outcome of the adjudication, then the nomination procedure to follow is the second one: *Party appointment*.
• The nomination procedure which is usually regarded as the best, because it ensures the complete independence and impartiality of the nominator, is the third one: *Appointment via an ANB*.

KEY POINT: *The best way to have an adjudicator nominated is by an Adjudicator Nominating Body.*

How is an adjudicator nominated by an ANB?

Many building contracts and contracts for the services of architects, quantity surveyors, engineers and others contain clauses that provide for disputes to be referred to adjudication. Frequently, the RIBA is named in these contracts as the ANB. Other ANBs include the Construction Industry Council, the Construction Confederation, the Institution of Civil Engineers, the Royal Institution of Chartered Surveyors, the Association for Consultancy and Engineering, the Association of Independent Construction Adjudicators, the Technology and Construction Solicitors Association and the Chartered Institute of Arbitrators.

The general procedure for the nomination of an adjudicator by an ANB is illustrated by that adopted by the RIBA. Where the right to adjudication is supplied by the Act (as amended), and the contract does not name the adjudicator, or an ANB other than the RIBA, then either party may apply by way of the RIBA standard application forms to the RIBA for it to nominate an adjudicator. A cheque for the administrative fee should accompany the completed forms.

See also: RIBA Application for Nomination of Adjudicator, page 51

From receipt of a completed application, the RIBA has up to seven days to nominate a suitable adjudicator from the RIBA President's List of Adjudicators, which includes architects, engineers, quantity surveyors and lawyers. The RIBA ensures that all those on the President's List are of the highest calibre, suitably qualified, trained, experienced and capable of discharging the duties of an adjudicator as well as having expertise in those subject areas for which the RIBA is likely to be asked to make a nomination.

The Adjudication Nomination Officer will approach a potential adjudicator on the RIBA List of Adjudicators to establish three things:

* *qualification* – that they have the relevant expertise to deal with the dispute
* *impartiality* – that they do not have any connection with the parties or the subject of the dispute which would disqualify them as an adjudicator
* *availability* – that they would be able to take the adjudication without delay.

If the potential adjudicator is able and willing to take the adjudication then they will be nominated. The RIBA will inform both parties of the fact, providing them with contact details for the adjudicator. The parties are asked to make contact with the adjudicator for directions.

See also: RIBA Nomination of Adjudicator, page 52

What happens when the adjudicator is nominated?

Immediately after their nomination, sometimes within a matter of hours, the adjudicator will contact both parties by way of introduction and to confirm the parties' contact details.

The adjudicator will normally write to the parties confirming the nomination, the adjudicator's terms of appointment and directions for the procedure and time-table of the adjudication. The adjudicator has 28 days to reach a decision from the date of receiving the Referral. The parties may, however, agree a longer period and the adjudicator, with the consent of the referring party, may extend the 28-day period by up to 14 days.

GOOD PRACTICE SUMMARY

- Make sure that a dispute has crystallised.
- Prepare the Notice of Adjudication carefully.
- Respond quickly.
- The best way to have an adjudicator nominated is by an Adjudicator Nominating Body.

Section 4
The adjudication

In this Section:

- *Introduction*
- *What are the powers of the adjudicator?*
- *Does the adjudicator have jurisdiction?*
- *What will the adjudicator do first?*
- *What is the Referral?*
- *What is the Response?*
- *Should I submit a Reply?*
- *Fairness*
- *Good practice summary*

Introduction

Adjudication, when used effectively and at the right time, can minimise delay and expense within a construction contract.

What are the powers of the adjudicator?

The powers of an adjudicator are wide, ranging from taking the initiative in ascertaining the facts and the law necessary to determine the dispute, to deciding the procedure to be followed in the adjudication. In carrying out the duties of the adjudication, the adjudicator must not only avoid incurring unnecessary expense but must also act impartially, in accordance with any relevant terms of the contract, and reach a decision in accordance with the applicable law in relation to the contract. Neither an adjudicator nor an employee or agent of an adjudicator is liable for anything done or omitted in the discharge or purported discharge of the functions of an adjudicator unless the act or omission is in bad faith.

29

An adjudicator may:

- request any party to the contract to supply documents which the adjudicator reasonably requires, including a written statement from any party to the contract supporting or supplementing the Referral Notice and any other documents that accompanied it on which the referring party intends to rely
- decide the language or languages to be used in the adjudication and whether a translation of any document is to be provided and, if so, by whom
- meet and question any of the parties to the contract and their representatives
- make appropriate site visits and inspections (subject to obtaining any necessary consent from third parties), either accompanied by the parties or not
- carry out any tests or experiments (subject to obtaining any necessary consent from third parties)
- obtain and consider representations and submissions which the adjudicator requires
- appoint experts, assessors or legal advisers (provided the adjudicator has notified the parties of his or her intention)
- give directions about the adjudication timetable, deadlines and limits on the length of written documents or oral representations
- issue other directions relating to the conduct of the adjudication.

The parties must comply with any request or direction of the adjudicator in relation to the adjudication. If a party does not do so without a sufficient reason then the adjudicator may:

- continue the adjudication in the absence of that party or of a document or written statement requested by the adjudicator
- draw such inferences from that failure to comply as circumstances may, in the adjudicator's opinion, justify
- make a decision on the basis of the information before the adjudicator, attaching such weight as the adjudicator thinks fit to any evidence submitted outside any directed period.

Does the adjudicator have jurisdiction?

Whether you are the referring party or the respondent, one of the most common issues which could affect you in an adjudication is a challenge to the jurisdiction of the adjudicator.

If you are the respondent then, by successfully challenging the adjudicator's jurisdiction, the adjudication is brought to an end, either entirely or for the part which has been successfully challenged. On the other hand, if you are the referring party then you need to be confident that the adjudicator has jurisdiction for the dispute you have referred. If the adjudicator acts without jurisdiction, any decision is worthless. Use the following points to double-check whether the adjudicator has jurisdiction:

- the contract is a construction contract[14] and is not an excluded contract (for example, one with a residential occupier) or, if it is an excluded contract,[15] that it specifically provides for adjudication to cover it
- the contract provides that if any dispute arises under the contract then either party to the contract may refer that dispute to adjudication in accordance with the requirements of the Act (as amended)[16] and valid rules are given for the conduct of an adjudication or, if not, then the Scheme for Construction Contracts applies
- the adjudicator has been appointed in accordance with the terms of the contract
- a dispute has crystallised
- the dispute and the redress summarised in the Notice of Adjudication are the same as those detailed in the Referral.

KEY POINT: *Double-check that the adjudicator has jurisdiction.*

What will the adjudicator do first?

After being nominated, an adjudicator will issue preliminary directions to the parties. Normally these will cover:

- the party by whom the adjudicator was nominated
- what documents the adjudicator has received from the ANB (for example, the referring party's Notice of Adjudication)

---

[14] Housing Grants, Construction and Regeneration Act 1996 (as amended), section 104.
[15] Housing Grants, Construction and Regeneration Act 1996 (as amended), sections 105(2), 106.
[16] Housing Grants, Construction and Regeneration Act 1996 (as amended), section 108.

- the adjudication agreement between the adjudicator and the parties, which should be completed and signed by each party and returned to the adjudicator – the adjudication agreement usually includes the terms and conditions of the adjudicator's appointment together with the fee basis on which the adjudicator proposes to charge
- the date by which the Referral Notice of the referring party should be received by the adjudicator. This should copied to the other party and should include:
    - the date by which the responding party should provide the adjudicator with a Response to the Referral Notice

See also: First Directions Letter, page 53

    - the date by which the Decision will be reached (i.e. within 28 days of the date the Referral was received by the adjudicator, excluding bank holidays and subject to any contractual or statutory extension of time).

KEY POINT: Keep a careful check on the dates by which things should be done, especially the date by which the Decision should be issued.

What is the Referral?

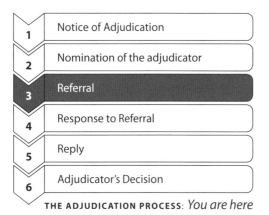

THE ADJUDICATION PROCESS: *You are here*

1 Notice of Adjudication
2 Nomination of the adjudicator
3 Referral
4 Response to Referral
5 Reply
6 Adjudicator's Decision

The Referral provides the detail only for those matters which have been summarised in the Notice of Adjudication. Usually the Notice of Adjudication and the Referral are written at the same time.

The date of the Referral (that is the date from which the Decision is calculated as being due) is the date on which the adjudicator receives the Referral.[17]

---

[17] In England, the Scheme for Construction Contracts (England and Wales) Regulations 1998 (Amendment) (England) Regulations 2011, regulation 3(7) amends paragraph 19(1) of the Scheme. Similarly, in Wales, the Scheme for Construction Contracts (England and Wales) Regulations 1998 (Amendment) (Wales) Regulations 2011 (Scheme for Construction Contracts (Wales) Regulations 2011), regulation 3(7) amends paragraph 19(1) of the Scheme.

The Referral should be as brief and concise as possible and include:

- a statement of the referring party's case set out in separately numbered paragraphs. It is good practice for this to cover the following:
  - *Introduction* – the names and contact details of the parties, their roles under the construction contract (e.g. employer, contractor, subcontractor) and a note of the way in which documents are referred to within the Referral and cross-referenced to a copy of that document attached as an appendix
  - *Contract* – the full name of the contract, its edition, amendments and date, together with any relevant documents that it incorporates (e.g. drawings, specification and bills of quantities), a summary of the obligations of the parties under the contract and relevant extracts from the contract
  - *Jurisdiction* – an explanation of why the contract is classified as a construction contract and why the adjudicator has jurisdiction, procedure to be followed in the adjudication (e.g. that of the Scheme for Construction Contracts or the Construction Industry Council Model Adjudication Procedure) and reasons for its selection, and the terms of the adjudication clause within the contract
  - *Dispute* – a description in chronological order of events in the dispute between the parties (i.e. the details of the circumstances giving rise to the dispute), the basis of the referring party's claim or position, what the referring party understands the position of the responding party to be and the reasons why the referring party is entitled to the redress sought
  - *Remedy* – the remedy that the referring party is seeking
- a copy of the contract
- the evidence upon which the referring party relies; for example, an architectural practice seeking outstanding fees may include:
  - statements of the practice's architects involved in the scheme explaining and providing details of the instructions, work done, the calculation of the claim and generally proving the documents produced in support of the claim
  - copies of the contract (if not already included in the Referral) or documents proving the existence of an oral contract, drawings produced, letters, meeting minutes, timesheets, submitted fee accounts, payment notices and any pay less notices[18]

---

[18] Housing Grants, Construction and Regeneration Act 1996 (as amended), sections 109 to 111.

See also:
Referral Notice, page 54

– a schedule of payments received and payments due.

Upon a dispute being referred to an adjudicator, the adjudicator informs the parties of the date of the Referral.[19]

What is the Response?

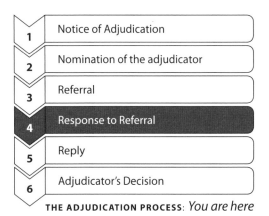

1 Notice of Adjudication

2 Nomination of the adjudicator

3 Referral

4 Response to Referral

5 Reply

6 Adjudicator's Decision

THE ADJUDICATION PROCESS: *You are here*

If you are the responding party, then your opportunity to explain your position to the adjudicator is provided by your Response to the referring party's Referral.

The Response should include:

• a concise statement (in numbered paragraphs) of the contentions on which the responding party relies; which allegations in each of the paragraphs in the Referral Notice the responding party admits, denies or is unable to admit or deny and requires the referring party to prove; if the allegation is denied, then the reasons for doing so, stating the responding party's version of events if this differs from that of the referring party

See also:
Response to Referral Notice, page 58

• any material that the responding party wishes the adjudicator to consider.

Should I submit a Reply?

As the referring party, you have a choice of whether or not to submit a Reply to the responding party's Response (subject to the discretion of the adjudicator to direct you to make a Reply).

---

[19] In England, the Scheme for Construction Contracts (England and Wales) Regulations 1998 (Amendment) (England) Regulations 2011, regulation 3(3). In Wales, the Scheme for Construction Contracts (England and Wales) Regulations 1998 (Amendment) (Wales) Regulations 2011 (Scheme for Construction Contracts (Wales) Regulations 2011), regulation 3(3).

1	Notice of Adjudication
2	Nomination of the adjudicator
3	Referral
4	Response to Referral
5	Reply
6	Adjudicator's Decision

THE ADJUDICATION PROCESS: *You are here*

A Reply may not be needed, unless the referring party wishes to allege facts in answer to the Response that were not included in the Referral Notice. Normally, unless the referring party makes an express admission, the responding party will have to prove the facts raised in its Response, whether or not a Reply is made by the referring party.

The referring party should not introduce any new issues into the adjudication via the Reply. It should not contradict or be inconsistent with the Referral Notice.

See also: Reply by the referring party, page 60

Fairness

In terms of evidence, the adjudicator may take the initiative in ascertaining the facts, as well as the law, necessary to determine the dispute, doing so in accordance with the applicable law in relation to the contract.

The standard of proof is the 'balance of probability'.

It is good practice for the rules of natural justice to be followed; that is, the emphasis is on fairness. This includes procedural fairness in giving both the respondent and the referring party the opportunity to be heard or present its evidence. Each party is entitled to ask questions and contradict the evidence of the other party. Only relevant considerations and extenuating circumstances should be taken into account. Irrelevant considerations should be ignored and justice should be seen to be done.

Practically, this requirement to apply the rules of natural justice means that:[20]

---

[20] In England, the Scheme for Construction Contracts (England and Wales) Regulations 1998 (Amendment) (England) Regulations 2011, regulations 16 to 18. In Wales, the Scheme for Construction Contracts (England and Wales) Regulations 1998 (Amendment) (Wales) Regulations 2011 (Scheme for Construction Contracts (Wales) Regulations 2011), regulations 16 to18.

- subject to any agreement between the parties to the contrary, any party to the dispute may be assisted by, or represented by, such advisers or representatives (whether legally qualified or not) as that party considers appropriate
- where the adjudicator is considering oral evidence or representations, a party to the dispute may not be represented by more than one person, unless the adjudicator gives directions to the contrary
- the adjudicator shall consider any relevant information submitted by any of the parties to the dispute and shall make available to them any information to be taken into account in reaching a decision
- the adjudicator and any party to the dispute shall not disclose to any other person any information or document provided to them in connection with the adjudication which the party supplying it has indicated is to be treated as confidential, except to the extent that it is necessary for the purposes of, or in connection with, the adjudication.

GOOD PRACTICE SUMMARY

- Double-check that the adjudicator has jurisdiction.
- Keep a careful check on the dates by which things should be done, especially the date by which the Decision should be issued.

Section 5
The adjudication Decision

In this Section:

- *Introduction*
- *How will a Decision be presented?*
- *Time frames for adjudicator's Decision*
- *Interest*
- *Who pays the costs of a party?*
- *Who pays the costs of the adjudicator?*
- *Complying with a Decision*
- *Good practice summary*

Introduction

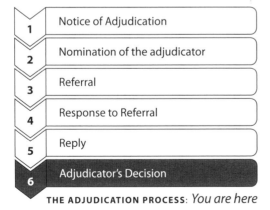

1	Notice of Adjudication
2	Nomination of the adjudicator
3	Referral
4	Response to Referral
5	Reply
6	Adjudicator's Decision

THE ADJUDICATION PROCESS: *You are here*

Of all the documents produced in the adjudication, one of the most important, if not the most important, is the *Decision* of the adjudicator. It determines whether or not the referring party has succeeded in the referral.

How will a Decision be presented?

The Decision can be given either with or without reasons.

The adjudicator must provide reasons for the Decision if requested by either party. There are both advantages and disadvantages in requesting reasons:

- you will be able to see whether or not the Decision has been reached fairly and reasonably by the adjudicator: if it has, then the Decision can be enforced quickly and effectively; if not, then the reasons given in the Decision will help you to decide whether to have the dispute decided afresh in arbitration or litigation
- a Decision with reasons costs more than a Decision without reasons as it will take the adjudicator longer to write and that additional time will be chargeable.

KEY POINT: It is good practice to ask for a reasoned Decision.

The starting point for a Decision is that the adjudicator must decide the matters in dispute: namely, those matters which have been set out in the Notice of Adjudication by the referring party.[21] In reaching a Decision an adjudicator may:

- take into account any other matters that the parties agree should be within the scope of the adjudication or that are matters under the contract which the adjudicator considers are necessarily connected with the dispute
- open up, revise and review any decision taken or any certificate given by any person referred to in the contract unless the contract states that the decision or certificate is final and conclusive
- decide that any of the parties to the dispute is liable to make a payment under the contract (whether in sterling or some other currency) and determine when that payment is due and the final date for payment.

---

[21] In England, the Scheme for Construction Contracts (England and Wales) Regulations 1998 (Amendment) (England) Regulations 2011, regulations 20 to 22. In Wales, the Scheme for Construction Contracts (England and Wales) Regulations 1998 (Amendment) (Wales) Regulations 2011 (Scheme for Construction Contracts (Wales) Regulations 2011), regulations 20 to 22.

A Decision may contain errors. The Scheme for Construction Contracts[22] provides that the adjudicator may, within five days of the Decision, correct the Decision so as to remove any error arising from a minor slip or omission.

See also: Decision, page 61

Time frames for adjudicator's Decision

A Decision must be reached by the adjudicator within one of the following time frames:[23]

- 28 days after the date on which the Referral was received by the adjudicator – the Construction Industry Council Model Adjudication Procedure states the date of referral to be the date on which the adjudicator receives the referring party's statement of case (which includes a copy of the Notice of Adjudication, the contract, details of the circumstances giving rise to the dispute, the reasons why it is entitled to the redress sought and the evidence on which it relies), or
- 42 days after the date of the referral notice if the referring party consents, or
- such period exceeding 28 days after the Referral Notice as the parties to the dispute may, after the giving of that notice, agree.

A copy of the Decision must be delivered by the adjudicator to both the referring party and the responding party as soon as possible after the Decision has been reached. An adjudicator cannot exercise a lien on the Decision to secure payment of his or her fees and expenses (a lien is the legal claim of one person upon the property of another person to secure the payment of a debt; so, for example, in an arbitration an arbitrator can refuse to issue the award until the parties have paid any outstanding money due to the arbitrator).

If, for any reason, a Decision is not reached by the adjudicator in accordance with any of the three time frames, then any of the parties to the dispute may serve a

---

[22] In England, the Scheme for Construction Contracts (England and Wales) Regulations 1998 (Amendment) (England) Regulations 2011, regulation 3(10). Similarly, in Wales, the Scheme for Construction Contracts (England and Wales) Regulations 1998 (Amendment) (Wales) Regulations 2011 (Scheme for Construction Contracts (Wales) Regulations 2011), regulation 3(10).

[23] Housing Grants, Construction and Regeneration Act 1996 (as amended), section 108(2).

fresh Notice of Adjudication for a new adjudicator to act. The parties should supply the new adjudicator (if requested and it is reasonably practicable) with copies of all documents which they had made available to the previous adjudicator.

KEY POINT: An adjudicator must deliver the Decision to the parties as soon as possible after it is made.

Interest

An adjudicator may decide (having regard to any term of the contract relating to the payment of interest) whether or not a party should pay interest. Such a decision could cover:

- the circumstances in which interest shall be paid
- the rates at which interest shall be paid
- the periods for which simple or compound rates of interest shall be paid.

Who pays the costs of a party?

There are a number of options relating to who pays the costs of a party to adjudication:

- the contract may provide that the parties shall bear their own costs and expenses incurred in the adjudication
- the parties may agree that the adjudicator shall decide which party shall pay costs and the amount of those costs
- the parties may make a written agreement after the appointment of the adjudicator allocating between themselves the costs relating to the adjudication. However, the agreement could be ineffective if the adjudicator determines that any of the costs (other than the adjudicator's fees or expenses) which a party is required to pay are unreasonable. Consequently, those costs would remain the responsibility of the party that incurred them. If a party disputes the adjudicator's determination then that party may apply to the court upon giving notice to the other party and the adjudicator. The court may then quash, uphold or vary the determination or substitute its own determination.

KEY POINT: Any contractual provision made between the parties which concerns the allocation between them of costs relating to the adjudication is ineffective unless:[24]

- *it is made in writing, is contained in the construction contract and confers power on the adjudicator to allocate his or her fees and expenses between the parties, or*
- *it is made in writing after the giving of a Notice of Adjudication.*

Who pays the costs of the adjudicator?

The adjudicator may look to all parties in the adjudication in order to recover the adjudicator's fees.

This means that if the adjudicator has made a Decision, or his or her appointment has been terminated (unless the termination is due to shortcomings or wrongdoing on the part of the adjudicator), then the parties are jointly and severally liable to pay the adjudicator a reasonable amount, determined by the adjudicator, in respect of fees for work reasonably undertaken and expenses reasonably incurred by the adjudicator. For example, if one party refuses to pay the adjudicator's fees then the adjudicator can seek payment from the other party.

KEY POINT: Remember that each party is jointly and severally liable to pay the adjudicator's fees.

Complying with a Decision

The parties must comply with the Decision of an adjudicator:

---

[24] Housing Grants, Construction and Regeneration Act 1996 (as amended), section 108A.

- *immediately* – if no date for performance has been directed by the adjudicator in the Decision (or if no date is to be implied by statute) then, on delivery of the Decision, the parties must comply with it immediately[25]
- within the time stipulated by the adjudicator in the Decision
- until the dispute is finally resolved by legal proceedings, by arbitration or by agreement. The parties are entitled to the redress set out in the Decision and to seek summary enforcement, whether or not the dispute is to be finally determined by legal proceedings or arbitration. No issue decided by the adjudicator may subsequently be referred for decision by another adjudicator unless so agreed by the parties.

---

[25] In England, the Scheme for Construction Contracts (England and Wales) Regulations 1998 (Amendment) (England) Regulations 2011, regulation 21. Similarly, in Wales, the Scheme for Construction Contracts (England and Wales) Regulations 1998 (Amendment) (Wales) Regulations 2011 (Scheme for Construction Contracts (Wales) Regulations 2011), regulation 21.

GOOD PRACTICE SUMMARY

- It is good practice to ask for a reasoned Decision.
- An adjudicator must deliver the Decision to the parties as soon as possible after it is made.
- Any contractual provision made between the parties which concerns the allocation between them of costs relating to the adjudication is ineffective unless:
  - it is made in writing, is contained in the construction contract and confers power on the adjudicator to allocate his or her fees and expenses between the parties, or
  - it is made in writing after the giving of a Notice of Adjudication.
- Remember that each party is jointly and severally liable to pay the adjudicator's fees.

Section 6
Adjudication letters and forms

In this Section:

Introduction
1. *Notice of Adjudication*
2. *RIBA Application for Nomination of Adjudicator*
3. *RIBA Nomination of Adjudicator*
4. *First Directions Letter*
5. *Referral Notice*
6. *Response to Referral Notice*
7. *Reply by the referring party*
8. *Decision*

Introduction

The letters and forms which are produced within adjudication usually follow a sequence from the first *Notice of Adjudication* through to the final *Decision* of the adjudicator. While there can be variations in the sequence as an adjudication progresses, the most common sequence of events and documents is:

- *Notice of Adjudication* from one party to the other. The details which it must contain are:
  - the nature and brief description of the dispute and the parties involved
  - when and where the dispute arose
  - the nature of the redress being sought
  - the names and addresses of the parties to the contract.
- The referring and responding parties may agree who the adjudicator is to be or which Adjudicator Nominating Body (ANB) is to nominate the adjudicator; for

example, they may be named in the contract, in which case the named adjudicator or ANB must be utilised. If the parties cannot agree, the named adjudicator is unable to accept the nomination or the contract does not identify which ANB is to be used, then an *Application for Nomination of Adjudicator* may be made to any ANB to nominate an adjudicator from its panel. The RIBA, the Chartered Institute of Arbitrators and the RICS, among others, are ANBs.

- *Nomination of Adjudicator* – the ANB will issue a notice to both parties informing them of the adjudicator whom it has nominated.
- *First Directions Letter* to the parties from the adjudicator upon nomination giving directions for the procedure and timetable of the adjudication. Also enclosed may be a *JCT Adjudication Agreement* and a *Schedule of Adjudicator's Fees.*
- *Referral Notice* from the referring party to the responding party and the adjudicator.
- *Response to Referral Notice* from the responding party to the referring party and the adjudicator.
- *Reply* by the referring party to the responding party and the adjudicator.
- *Decision* by the adjudicator.

Some examples of these adjudication letters and forms follow.

1. Notice of Adjudication

See Section 3, Starting adjudication: made easy – What should a Notice of Adjudication contain?

Adjudication reference: …

IN THE MATTER OF THE HOUSING GRANTS, CONSTRUCTION AND REGENERATION ACT 1996 (as amended)

AND IN THE MATTER OF AN ADJUDICATION

BETWEEN:

AB LLP   *Referring party*

and

CD LIMITED   *Responding party*

NOTICE OF ADJUDICATION

Dispute

1. By a Memorandum of Agreement dated … the referring party and the responding party entered into a contract (in the form of …) in relation to the appointment of the referring party to provide architectural and contract administration services in connection with the development of houses owned by the responding party at … *(address)*.

2. In accordance with the terms of the contract the referring party submitted nine invoices between … and … to the responding party seeking payment of the total sum of £ …

3. Wrongly and in breach of contract, the responding party has failed to pay any of the invoices.

Redress

4. The referring party seeks the following redress:

    i.   A Decision that the responding party pays the referring party the sum of £ … or such other sum as the adjudicator considers fit within seven days of the date of the Decision.

    ii. A Decision that the responding party pays interest on any sum awarded by the adjudicator at the rate of … % over the Bank of England base rate from the date of the final date for payment of each invoice pursuant to clause … of the contract.

    iii. A Decision that the responding party pays the adjudicator's fees and expenses incurred in this adjudication.

Parties

5. The names and addresses for service of the parties are as follows:

AB LLP
... *(address)*
Referring party

Address for service:
MN Solicitors LLP, ... *(address)*
Tel: ... Fax: ... Email: ...
Ref: ...

CD Ltd
... *(address)*
Responding party

Address for service:
OP Solicitors LLP, ... *(address)*
Tel: ... Fax: ... Email: ...
Ref: ...

Dated ...

(Signed) ...
(Name and address of the referring party/representative) ...

2. RIBA Application for Nomination of Adjudicator

See Section 3, Starting adjudication: made easy – How is an adjudicator nominated by an ANB?

Royal Institute of British Architects, 66 Portland Place, London W1B 1AD

FORM OF APPLICATION FOR NOMINATION OF A PERSON TO ACT AS ADJUDICATOR

Regarding the agreement dated the .... day of ...., 20 ....(the Contract) and made between

....of the one part

and

....of the other part

Whereas

1.   a dispute or difference has arisen under the Contract
2.   the applicant is entitled to refer the dispute or difference to the adjudication of a person nominated by the RIBA/President of the RIBA
3.   a notice of adjudication has been given to the other party

I/We hereby apply to the **RIBA / President of the RIBA**** for the nomination of a person to act as adjudicator *and enclose* a copy of the above mentioned notice of adjudication together with a cheque (made out to "Royal Institute of British Architects") for the Administration Fee of £240 plus VAT (or £115 inclusive of VAT for disputes arising under the JCT Building Contract for a Home Owner/Occupier). On receipt of payment, a receipted invoice will be sent directly to the applicant.

STATEMENT OF PARTICULARS

Name and address of applicant: Name and address of other party:

Telephone: Telephone:
Fax: Fax:

Name of Architect/Contract Administrator (if any) ....

Brief outline of the matter in dispute (e.g. quality of workmanship, claim for extension of time, valuation of works, entitlement to fees):
....
....

Where the dispute has arisen (location):
....

The Contract is** / is not** a standard form issued by the Joint Contracts Tribunal (JCT).

If JCT Contract, state which form ....

Signed* : .... Date: ....

Print Name: ....

*   *The name of a signatory must be legibly printed under the signature and the signatory if not the applicant must be authorised to sign on behalf of the applicant.*
**   *Delete as applicable*

DISCLAIMER
The RIBA, its servants or agents, shall not be liable for anything done or omitted in respect of this application unless the act or omission is shown to have been in bad faith and shall not be liable for anything done or omitted by any person nominated, his servants or agents, whether in the discharge or purported discharge of his functions as adjudicator or otherwise.

3. RIBA Nomination of Adjudicator

See Section 3, Starting adjudication: made easy – How is an adjudicator nominated by an ANB?

RIBA ♯♯

NOMINATION OF A PERSON TO ACT AS ADJUDICATOR
In the matter of a dispute between......................

In response to the application dated ....* by ....for the nomination of a person to act as adjudicator

Nominated Person

....

is hereby nominated adjudicator

Signed on behalf of the President...(....................)

Dated: ....

*copy attached

4. First Directions Letter

See Section 4, The adjudication – What will the adjudicator do first?

By email or by post and email

Adjudication reference: …

AB Partnership	CD Limited
…	…
(Name and address of the referring party/representative)	*(Name and address of the responding party/representative)*
Attention: …	Attention: …
Reference: …	Reference: …
Referring party	**Responding party**

Dear Sirs,

Adjudication between AB Partnership and CD Limited

I have been nominated by the President of the Royal Institute of British Architects to act as adjudicator in this adjudication.

I have received a copy of the Notice of Intention to Refer a Dispute to Adjudication dated … of the referring party, AB Ltd, from which I note that the contract between the parties is the … . Please find attached the JCT Adjudication Agreement for completion and signature by each party which should then be returned to me.

I look forward to receiving by … the Referral Notice on behalf of the referring party which should be simultaneously copied to the other party and should include:

1. a statement of its case
2. a copy of the contract
3. details of the circumstances giving rise to the dispute
4. the reasons why it is entitled to the redress sought
5. the evidence upon which it relies.

Within seven days of the date of the Referral Notice the responding party may send to myself:

1. a written statement of the contentions on which it relies
2. any material that it wishes me to consider.

It would be most helpful if a copy of the text of the main submissions were emailed to me at … *(email address)*.

A Decision will be reached by …, that is within 28 days of the date on which I receive the Referral, subject to any contractual or statutory extension of time.

Yours faithfully,

… *(Signed)*
Adjudicator

5. Referral Notice

See Section 4, The adjudication – What is the Referral?

Adjudication reference: ...

IN THE MATTER OF THE HOUSING GRANTS, CONSTRUCTION AND REGENERATION ACT 1996 (as amended)

AND IN THE MATTER OF AN ADJUDICATION

BETWEEN:

AB COUNTY BOROUGH COUNCIL   *Referring party*

and

CD CONSTRUCTION LIMITED   *Responding party*

<u>**REFERRAL**</u>

Introduction

1. The referring party is AB County Borough Council ('the Council') whose address is ...

2. The responding party is CD Construction Limited ('CD') whose registered office is situated at ...

3. Pursuant to a dispute between the parties, more fully particularised in a Notice of Adjudication dated ..., the Council hereby refers the dispute to adjudication in accordance with the terms of the contract.

4. Where documents and correspondence are referred to within this Referral, the relevant documents and correspondence are appended to the Referral Notice in the Appendix. References to sections and/or page numbers in square brackets within this document refer to corresponding sections and/or page numbers within the Appendix.

Contract

5. The contract is a JCT Standard Form of Building Contract with Contractor's Design ... Edition incorporating Amendments 1 to ... and bespoke amendments agreed between the parties dated ...

6. The contract obliges CD to undertake the design and construction of a five-storey council office building, together with ancillary infrastructure and landscaping works, at ...

7. The contract incorporates the Employer's Requirements and the Contractor's Proposals, which include, among other things, the following documents:

    i.   Employer's Requirements Performance Specification Volume 1 – Section 3 (3.5) Electrical Services Specification.

    ii. Employer's Requirements Performance Specification Volume 2 – Appendix CC Mechanical & Electrical Services Room Data Sheets Issue 4 Revision 1. The Room Data Sheets were updated and re-issued to CD during the course of the tender process as a separate document to the original tender information.

iii. Contractor's Proposals – Amendments to Contractor's Proposals – Post Tender. The Room Data Sheets contained within the Post Tender Amendments are variations to the Room Data Sheets requested by the Council in ... following CD's successful tender.

Jurisdiction

8. The adjudicator has jurisdiction in that:

Contract

i. The contract between the parties is a construction contract in accordance with the provisions of section 104 of the *Housing Grants, Construction and Regeneration Act 1996* (as amended) and is not subject to any of the exclusions set out at sections 105(2) or 106 of the Act.

ii. The contract is:
- partly in writing by the documents referred to above
- partly oral by a meeting held between the parties on ... at ....

iii. In accordance with the requirements of the *Housing Grants, Construction and Regeneration Act 1996* (as amended) section 108, Article ... of the contract provides that if any dispute or difference arises under the contract then either party to the contract may refer that dispute to adjudication.

iv. Clause ... of the contract sets out valid rules for the conduct of any such adjudication.

Appointment

v. No specific adjudicator is named under the contract. The contract provides that where either party refers a dispute to adjudication, the adjudicator is to be nominated by the Royal Institute of British Architects.

vi. The Council has made an appropriate application to the Royal Institute of British Architects and the adjudicator has been appointed by the Royal Institute of British Architects in accordance with the terms of the contract.

Dispute

vii. In ... the parties identified a discrepancy between the number of floor outlet boxes ('Floor Boxes') the Council expected to be installed at AB House under the contract and the number of Floor Boxes that CD expected to install.

viii. The parties have sought to resolve the issue of the number of Floor Boxes to be installed through the process of negotiation. However, the parties have been unable to resolve this issue and an impasse has been reached which does not appear capable of resolution at the present time.

ix. On the basis that the parties have reached an impasse the Council submits that a dispute has crystallised between the parties which may be referred to adjudication for resolution.

9. The contract is a construction contract partly evidenced in writing and partly oral, the adjudicator has been appointed in accordance with the terms of the contract and a dispute has arisen between the parties. Consequently, the adjudicator has jurisdiction to make a decision in respect of this dispute.

Dispute

10. On ..., the Council issued Employer's Change Requirement 17. The Employer's Change Requirement process is a mechanism which permits the parties to consider the probable cost and time implications of a suggested variation to the Employer's Requirements prior to the employer issuing a formal instruction. ECR 17 evidenced the Council's wish to change its Floor Box requirements to 903 Floor Boxes.

11. CD responded substantively to ECR 17 on ..., stating that the amended number of Floor Boxes would have no effect on the contract period but would mean an addition to the contract sum of £111,009.50. The parties realised that they had a different understanding as to the number of Floor Boxes that CD was to provide under the contract.

12. The Council's interpretation of the contract when the dispute arose was that CD was required to supply and install 967 Floor Boxes in accordance with the Room Data Sheets as varied by the Post Tender Amendments.

13. CD denied that it was obliged to supply and install 967 Floor Boxes and asserted that it was only required to supply and install 530 Floor Boxes in accordance with its interpretation of the Electrical Specification AB01-6505.

14. While the Council disputed CD's interpretation of AB01-6505, in order to allow progress on site the Council issued on ... Employer's Instruction 53 and the completed ECR 17. These documents instructed CD to install 903 Floor Boxes with the costs to be agreed.

15. The parties discussed the Floor Box issue and exchanged correspondence. Following receipt of CD's letter of ... which confirmed that CD had tendered to install 536 Floor Boxes (not 530) and that CD was taking external advice, the Council took legal advice on its position and on the interpretation of AB01-6505.

16. Following receipt of this advice, the Council amended its position to confirm that on a correct reading of AB01-6505 CD was obliged to supply and install 1,361 Floor Boxes. The Council's amended position was set out in its letter of ...

17. The Council sent a final letter on ... confirming that as CD had not accepted the Council's position set out in its letter of ... and given that this matter had remained unresolved since ..., a dispute had arisen between the parties.

Basis of claim

18. The Electrical Specification AB01-6505 states, at paragraph 13, that the tendering parties are required to:

'Install floor outlet boxes on the basis of one per two workstations on the upper floors. For tender purposes, assume 200 workstations per upper floor area, evenly distributed. In addition, provide power outlets to ground floor and other specific areas, as defined on the Room Data Sheets.'

Council's position

19. The Council considers the requirements of paragraph 13 of AB01-6505 are clear and unambiguous. On the natural interpretation of this paragraph, CD is obliged to supply and install 1,361 Floor Boxes calculated on the following basis:

    i.   one per every two workstations on the upper floors, equating to 100 Floor Boxes on each of the 1st, 2nd, 3rd and 4th floors (400 Floor Boxes); and in addition

ii.   the number of Floor Boxes specified in the Room Data Sheets. The Council calculates that the Room Data Sheets require CD to supply and install 961 Floor Boxes as set out in the Council's Floor Box Calculation.

CD's position

20. CD disputes the Council's interpretation of AB01-6505 and asserts that it is only obliged to supply and install 536 Floor Boxes. This figure is calculated on the basis that AB01-6505 obliges CD to supply 400 Floor Boxes to the upper floors and additional Floor Boxes to the ground floor and upper floors as defined in the Room Data Sheets but excluding those Room Data Sheets which relate to the workstation areas of the upper floors.

Remedy

21. The Council invites the adjudicator to decide as follows:

i.   that CD is obliged under the contract to provide 1,361 Floor Boxes or such other number of Floor Boxes as the adjudicator may decide; and

ii.   that CD pays all of the adjudicator's fees and expenses.

Dated: . . .

(Signed) . . .

(Name and address of the referring party/representative) . . .

6. Response to Referral Notice

See Section 4, The adjudication – What is the Response?

Adjudication reference: ...

IN THE MATTER OF THE HOUSING GRANTS, CONSTRUCTION AND REGENERATION ACT 1996 (as amended)

AND IN THE MATTER OF AN ADJUDICATION

BETWEEN:

AB ARCHITECTURAL PARTNERSHIP   *Referring party*

and

MR CD   *Responding party*

RESPONSE TO REFERRAL NOTICE

1. The responding party, Mr CD, adopts the paragraph reference numbers in the referring party, AB Architectural Partnership, Referral Notice.

Jurisdiction

2. Mr CD challenges the jurisdiction of the adjudicator to act in this matter because:

    Adjudicator's appointment

    i.   AB Architectural Partnership's letter dated ... to Mr CD stated that they had that day made a reference to adjudication, '*pursuant to the ... (contract) clause ... to refer this dispute to adjudication in accordance with the Construction Industry Council Model Adjudication Procedure ... '*. The letter was in breach of the requirements of contract clause ... that, '*Where no adjudicator is named in the Appointment and the parties are unable to agree on a person to act as adjudicator, the adjudicator shall be a person to be appointed at the request of either party by the nominator identified in the Letter of Appointment'*. In breach of clause ... no nominator was named in the letter of appointment dated ...

    Dispute or difference

    ii. For there to be a valid adjudication there must be a dispute or difference. No dispute or difference has arisen and this adjudication is not valid because on ... Mr CD wrote to AB Architectural Partnership questioning the amount and type of services it had provided for the fees paid. Without further discussion between the parties, AB Architectural Partnership began adjudication immediately.

Evidence

3. Paragraph 1 of the Referral Notice is denied by Mr CD. The claim of AB Architectural Partnership has not been previously presented to Mr CD. It is unsupported by any evidence. Mr CD does not know to what extent AB Architectural Partnership has actually carried out work in connection with RIBA Work Stage D. No drawings or

---

detailed time sheets have been provided by the architects. Furthermore, any progression to Work Stage D by AB Architectural Partnership was without the permission of Mr CD.

4.   ... *(Continue through each paragraph of the referring party's Referral Notice setting out the responding party's case and summarising any relevant supporting evidence. If the evidence is taken from a document then that document should be attached in an appendix to the Response to the Referral Notice unless it has already been provided by the referring party in its Referral Notice).*

5.   Except as is expressly admitted or not admitted, each and every allegation in AB Architectural Partnership's Referral Notice is denied as if it were set out and expressly traversed.

Dated: ...

(Signed) ...

(Name and address of the responding party/representative) ...

7. Reply by the referring party

See Section 4, The adjudication – Should I submit a Reply?

Adjudication reference: ...

IN THE MATTER OF THE HOUSING GRANTS, CONSTRUCTION AND REGENERATION ACT 1996 (as amended)

AND IN THE MATTER OF AN ADJUDICATION

BETWEEN:

AB ARCHITECTS LLP   *Referring party*

and

MR CD   *Responding party*

REPLY BY THE REFERRING PARTY
TO THE RESPONDING PARTY'S RESPONSE TO THE REFERRAL NOTICE

Contract

1. The crux of Mr CD's contentions in his *Responding Party's Response to the Referral Notice* paragraphs ... to ... is that he had rejected the ... contract, there were oral discussions between the parties for the provision of architectural services by the referring party, AB Architects LLP, but no agreement had been reached between them which amounted to a construction contract within the meaning of the *Housing Grants, Construction and Regeneration Act 1996* (as amended).

2. AB Architects LLP deny the *Responding Party's Response to the Referral Notice* because:

    i.   The contract contemplates that the architects' fees will be paid on the basis either of a percentage or of time.

    ii. The only element in the architects' emailed offer dated ... which Mr CD objected to in a telephone conversation with the architects on ... was the payment of fees on a percentage basis. It was changed by agreement by substituting the provision for fees to be paid on a time basis.

    iii. Mr CD did not reject the architects' entire offer. He has never indicated that the remaining provisions of the ... contract were unacceptable and were not to be used.

    iv. Mr CD had previous experience of retaining architects, so would not be surprised to see that an RIBA standard contract was referred to in AB Architects LLP's offer and would know that if he were to refuse to contract by reference to such a contract, he would be unlikely to find any architect to act for him.

3. AB Architects LLP proceeded to provide professional services in accordance with the instructions of Mr CD which were invoiced on a time basis as set out in the architects' *Referral Notice*.

Dated: ...

(Signed) ...

(Name and address of the referring party/representative) ...

---

8. Decision

See Section 5, The adjudication Decision – How will a Decision be presented?

Adjudication reference: ...

IN THE MATTER OF THE HOUSING GRANTS, CONSTRUCTION AND REGENERATION ACT 1996 (as amended)

AND IN THE MATTER OF AN ADJUDICATION

BETWEEN:

MR AND MRS AB   *Referring party*

and

CD ARCHITECTS LIMITED   *Responding party*

<u>**DECISION**</u>

Nomination

1. I, ..., was nominated by the parties pursuant to the parties' letter dated ... to act as adjudicator in a dispute which has arisen between Mr and Mrs AB and CD Architects Ltd under a contract in the form of ... issued by the Joint Contracts Tribunal Ltd and dated ... (referred to as, 'the contract form'). The contract was between Mr and Mrs AB and EF Construction Ltd, a company now in liquidation. The architect was named in the contract as JH Architects who were replaced on ... by CD Architects Ltd. The contract was for the refurbishment of a hotel owned by Mr and Mrs AB at ...

Documents

2. I have received and considered the parties' Joint Referral Document, dated ... and supporting documents.

3. On ... I invited the parties to confirm whether they wished to have the opportunity to reply to the contractual position of the other party. On ... each party confirmed that they did not wish to do so.

Jurisdiction

4. The parties in the Joint Referral Document acknowledge and consent to my having jurisdiction to decide upon the following dispute.

Dispute

5. In the Joint Referral Document the parties state that the dispute concerns the following issues:

     i.   What documentation falls within the contract?

     ii.   ... *(all other issues are set out)*.

Redress

6. The parties seek the following redress:

i.   A declaration as to the scope of documentation forming the contract.

ii.   ... *(all other redress is set out).*

7.   The parties request reasons to be given.

Contract documents

8.   Mr and Mrs AB maintain that the documentation which falls within the contract comprises the contract form, the drawings listed on JH Architects' drawings issue sheet dated ... and JH Architects' Preliminary Cost Plan dated ...

9.   CD Architects Ltd maintains that only the contract form is a contract document. The drawings are not signed as contract drawings and they suspect JH Architects' drawings issue sheet reference was added after the contract was signed because the contractor's managing director, Mr L, in his statement dated ... indicates he did not have sight of the drawings before signing the contract. Also JH Architects' Preliminary Cost Plan contained budget costs, *'prepared in accordance with General Layout Plans numbered 04 and 05 dated ... ',* which became provisional sums post contract.

10.   I decide that the scope of the documentation forming the contract is the contract form dated ... and also listed on JH Architects' drawings issue sheet dated ... because:

i.   It is common ground that the contract form is a contract document; it is signed as such on behalf of the employer and the contractor.

ii.   The drawings are referred to within the contract as contract drawings. The contract form clause ... states, ' ... *drawings numbered see issue sheet dated ... (hereinafter called the "Contract Drawings")'.* Also it appears from Mr L's statement that the contract form was signed on behalf of the contractor by Mr L after he had discussed this reference to the drawings with JH Architects although he had not seen all those drawings. As mentioned on behalf of Mr and Mrs AB, a party signing a contract will ordinarily be bound by the terms of the agreement whether or not he or she has read them and whether or not he or she is ignorant of their precise legal effect.

iii.   The contract does not list the Preliminary Cost Plan as a contract document either under clause ... or under any other clause. I note it is common ground that the document may be used as an evidential aid to construction of the contract documents.

11.   .... *(all other issues and relevant evidence are set out and dealt with).*

Costs

12.   By the Schedule of Adjudicators Fees signed by the parties on ... (being the day after the parties jointly nominated myself as adjudicator) it was provided, *'Each party shall pay to the adjudicator an equal proportion of the adjudicator's fees and expenses'*, and I so direct.

Decision

13.   **I NOW** having considered the submissions of the parties and the documents provided to me, **HEREBY DECIDE AND DECLARE**:

i.   The scope of the documentation forming the contract is:

a. The contract form … issued by the Joint Contracts Tribunal Ltd and dated …

b. The drawings listed on JH Architects' drawings issue sheet dated …

ii. *(The decisions on all other issues are set down).*

iii. The referring party and the responding party shall each pay 50 per cent of my fees in this adjudication which I assess at … (£ … plus VAT at … % of £ …), such payment shall be made by …. I further direct that if one party fails to pay the fees as directed then the other party shall pay those fees and recover payment of those fees as monies recoverable in this adjudication.

Dated …

(Signed) …
Adjudicator

Section 7
Further reading

The classic legal book on adjudication is Peter Coulson's *Coulson on Construction Adjudication*, second edition (Oxford University Press, March 2011).

Websites where you can find more details about court procedures, acts, statutory instruments and cases are as follows:

- www.justice.gov.uk/civil/procrules
  This Ministry of Justice website contains the most up-to-date court rules, practice directions, forms and guides.
- www.legislation.gov.uk
  The website which is delivered by the National Archives contains comprehensive UK legislation and statutory instruments.
- www.bailii.org
  The British and Irish Legal Information Institute website provides access to freely available British and Irish case law and legislation, European Union case law and Law Commission reports.

Both Mair Coombes Davies' *RIBA Good Practice Guide: Arbitration* and Andrzej Grossman's *RIBA Good Practice Guide: Mediation* provide introductory information on other dispute resolution procedures, while following the advice given in Owen Luder's *RIBA Good Practice Guide: Keeping out of Trouble* will hopefully reduce the chances of having to consult a book about disputes in the first place.

Appendix 1

The Housing Grants, Construction and Regeneration Act 1996 as amended by the Local Democracy, Economic Development and Construction Act 2009

PART II CONSTRUCTION CONTRACTS

Introductory provisions

104 Construction contracts

(1) In this Part a "construction contract" means an agreement with a person for any of the following—
   (a) the carrying out of construction operations;
   (b) arranging for the carrying out of construction operations by others, whether under sub-contract to him or otherwise;
   (c) providing his own labour, or the labour of others, for the carrying out of construction operations.

(2) References in this Part to a construction contract include an agreement—
   (a) to do architectural, design, or surveying work, or
   (b) to provide advice on building, engineering, interior or exterior decoration or on the laying-out of landscape,
in relation to construction operations.

(3) References in this Part to a construction contract do not include a contract of employment (within the meaning of the Employment Rights Act 1996).

(4) The Secretary of State may by order add to, amend or repeal any of the provisions of subsection (1), (2) or (3) as to the agreements which are construction contracts for the purposes of this Part or are to be taken or not to be taken as included in references to such contracts.

No such order shall be made unless a draft of it has been laid before and approved by a resolution of each of House of Parliament.

(5) Where an agreement relates to construction operations and other matters, this Part applies to it only so far as it relates to construction operations.

An agreement relates to construction operations so far as it makes provision of any kind within subsection (1) or (2).

(6) This Part applies only to construction contracts which—

(a) are entered into after the commencement of this Part, and

(b) relate to the carrying out of construction operations in England, Wales or Scotland.

(7) This Part applies whether or not the law of England and Wales or Scotland is otherwise the applicable law in relation to the contract.

105 Meaning of ''construction operations''

(1) In this Part ''construction operations'' means, subject as follows, operations of any of the following descriptions—

(a) construction, alteration, repair, maintenance, extension, demolition or dismantling of buildings, or structures forming, or to form, part of the land (whether permanent or not);

(b) construction, alteration, repair, maintenance, extension, demolition or dismantling of any works forming, or to form, part of the land, including (without prejudice to the foregoing) walls, roadworks, power-lines, electronic communication apparatus, aircraft runways, docks and harbours, railways, inland waterways, pipe-lines, reservoirs, water-mains, wells, sewers, industrial plant and installations for purposes of land drainage, coast protection or defence;

(c) installation in any building or structure of fittings forming part of the land, including (without prejudice to the foregoing) systems of heating, lighting, air-conditioning, ventilation, power supply, drainage, sanitation, water supply or fire protection, or security or communications systems;

(d) external or internal cleaning of buildings and structures, so far as carried out in the course of their construction, alteration, repair, extension or restoration;

(e) operations which form an integral part of, or are preparatory to, or are for rendering complete, such operations as are previously described in this subsection, including site clearance, earth-moving, excavation, tunnelling and boring, laying of foundations, erection, maintenance or dismantling of scaffolding, site restoration, landscaping and the provision of roadways and other access works;

(f) painting or decorating the internal or external surfaces of any building or structure.

(2) The following operations are not construction operations within the meaning of this Part—

(a) drilling for, or extraction of, oil or natural gas;

(b) extraction (whether by underground or surface working) of minerals; tunnelling or boring, or construction of underground works, for this purpose;

(c) assembly, installation or demolition of plant or machinery, or erection or demolition of steelwork for the purposes of supporting or providing access to plant or machinery, on a site where the primary activity is—

(i) nuclear processing, power generation, or water or effluent treatment, or

(ii) the production, transmission, processing or bulk storage (other than warehousing) of chemicals, pharmaceuticals, oil, gas, steel or food and drink;

(d) manufacture or delivery to site of—

(i) building or engineering components or equipment,

(ii) materials, plant or machinery, or

(iii) components for systems of heating, lighting, air-conditioning, ventilation, power supply, drainage, sanitation, water supply or fire protection, or for security or communications systems,

except under a contract which also provides for their installation;

(e) the making, installation and repair of artistic works, being sculptures, murals and other works which are wholly artistic in nature.

(3) The Secretary of State may by order add to, amend or repeal any of the provisions of subsection (1) or (2) as to the operations and work to be treated as construction operations for the purposes of this Part.

(4) No such order shall be made unless a draft of it has been laid before and approved by a resolution of each House of Parliament.

106 Provisions not applicable to contract with residential occupier

(1) This Part does not apply—

　　(a) to a construction contract with a residential occupier (see below).

(2) A construction contract with a residential occupier means a construction contract which principally relates to operations on a dwelling which one of the parties to the contract occupies, or intends to occupy, as his residence.

　　In this subsection "dwelling" means a dwelling-house or a flat; and for this purpose—

　　　　"dwelling-house" does not include a building containing a flat; and

　　　　"flat" means separate and self-contained premises constructed or adapted for use for residential purposes and forming part of a building from some other part of which the premises are divided horizontally.

(3) The Secretary of State may by order amend subsection (2).

(4) No order under this section shall be made unless a draft of it has been laid before and approved by a resolution of each House of Parliament.

106A Power to disapply provisions of this Part

(1) The Secretary of State may by order provide that any or all of the provisions of this Part, so far as extending to England and Wales, shall not apply to any description of construction contract relating to the carrying out of construction operations (not being operations in Wales) which is specified in the order.

(2) The Welsh Ministers may by order provide that any or all of the provisions of this Part, so far as extending to England and Wales, shall not apply to any description of construction contract relating to the carrying out of construction operations in Wales which is specified in the order.

(3) The Scottish Ministers may by order provide that any or all of the provisions of this Part, so far as extending to Scotland, shall not apply to any description of construction contract which is specified in the order.

(4) An order under this section shall not be made unless a draft of it has been laid before and approved by resolution of—

(a) in the case of an order under subsection (1), each House of Parliament;

(b) in the case of an order under subsection (2), the National Assembly for Wales;

(c) in the case of an order under subsection (3), the Scottish Parliament.

107 [Deleted].

Adjudication

108 Right to refer disputes to adjudication

(1) A party to a construction contract has the right to refer a dispute arising under the contract for adjudication under a procedure complying with this section.

For this purpose "dispute" includes any difference.

(2) The contract shall include provision in writing so as to—

(a) enable a party to give notice at any time of his intention to refer a dispute to adjudication;

(b) provide a timetable with the object of securing the appointment of the adjudicator and referral of the dispute to him within 7 days of such notice;

(c) require the adjudicator to reach a decision within 28 days of referral or such longer period as is agreed by the parties after the dispute has been referred;

(d) allow the adjudicator to extend the period of 28 days by up to 14 days, with the consent of the party by whom the dispute was referred;

(e) impose a duty on the adjudicator to act impartially; and

(f) enable the adjudicator to take the initiative in ascertaining the facts and the law.

(3) The contract shall provide in writing that the decision of the adjudicator is binding until the dispute is finally determined by legal proceedings, by arbitration (if the contract provides for arbitration or the parties otherwise agree to arbitration) or by agreement.

The parties may agree to accept the decision of the adjudicator as finally determining the dispute.

(3A) The contract shall include provision in writing permitting the adjudicator to correct his decision so as to remove a clerical or typographical error arising by accident or omission.

(4)   The contract shall also provide in writing that the adjudicator is not liable for anything done or omitted in the discharge or purported discharge of his functions as adjudicator unless the act or omission is in bad faith, and that any employee or agent of the adjudicator is similarly protected from liability.

(5)   If the contract does not comply with the requirements of subsections (1) to (4), the adjudication provisions of the Scheme for Construction Contracts apply.

(6)   For England and Wales, the Scheme may apply the provisions of the Arbitration Act 1996 with such adaptations and modifications as appear to the Minister making the scheme to be appropriate.
      For Scotland, the Scheme may include provision conferring powers on courts in relation to adjudication and provision relating to the enforcement of the adjudicator's decision.

108A Adjudication costs: effectiveness of provision

(1)   This section applies in relation to any contractual provision made between the parties to a construction contract which concerns the allocation as between those parties of costs relating to the adjudication of a dispute arising under the construction contract.

(2)   The contractual provision referred to in subsection (1) is ineffective unless—

(a)   it is made in writing, is contained in the construction contract and confers power on the adjudicator to allocate his fees and expenses as between the parties, or

(b)   it is made in writing after the giving of notice of intention to refer the dispute to adjudication.

109 Entitlement to stage payments

(1)   A party to a construction contract is entitled to payment by instalments, stage payments or other periodic payments for any work under the contract unless—

(a)   it is specified in the contract that the duration of the work is to be less than 45 days, or

     (b)   it is agreed between the parties that the duration of the work is estimated to be less than 45 days.

(2)   The parties are free to agree the amounts of the payments and the intervals at which, or circumstances in which, they become due.

(3)   In the absence of such agreement, the relevant provisions of the Scheme for Construction Contracts apply.

(4)   References in the following sections to a payment provided for by the contract include a payment by virtue of this section.

110 Dates for payment

(1)   Every construction contract shall—

     (a)   provide an adequate mechanism for determining what payments become due under the contract, and when, and

     (b)   provide for a final date for payment in relation to any sum which becomes due.

   The parties are free to agree how long the period is to be between the date on which a sum becomes due and the final date for payment.

(1A)   The requirement in subsection (1)(a) to provide an adequate mechanism for determining what payments become due under the contract, or when, is not satisfied where a construction contract makes payment conditional on—

     (a)   the performance of obligations under another contract, or

     (b)   a decision by any person as to whether obligations under another contract have been performed.

(1B)   In subsection (1A)(a) and (b) the references to obligations do not include obligations to make payments (but see section 113).

(1C)   Subsection (1A) does not apply where—

     (a)   the construction contract is an agreement between the parties for the carrying out of construction operations by another person, whether under sub-contract or otherwise, and

     (b)   the obligations referred to in that subsection are obligations on that other person to carry out those operations.

(1D)   The requirement in subsection (1)(a) to provide an adequate mechanism for determining when payments become due under the contract is not satisfied where a construction contract provides for the date on which a payment becomes due to be determined by reference to the giving to the person to whom the payment is due of a notice which relates to what payments are due under the contract.

(2)   [Deleted].

(3)   If or to the extent that a contract does not contain such provision as is mentioned in subsection (1), the relevant provisions of the Scheme for Construction Contracts apply.

110A Payment notices: contractual requirements

(1)   A construction contract shall, in relation to every payment provided for by the contract—

    (a)   require the payer or a specified person to give a notice complying with subsection (2) to the payee not later than five days after the payment due date, or

    (b)   require the payee to give a notice complying with subsection (3) to the payer or a specified person not later than five days after the payment due date.

(2)   A notice complies with this subsection if it specifies—

    (a)   in a case where the notice is given by the payer—

        (i)   the sum that the payer considers to be or to have been due at the payment due date in respect of the payment, and

        (ii)   the basis on which that sum is calculated;

    (b)   in a case where the notice is given by a specified person—

        (i)   the sum that the payer or the specified person considers to be or to have been due at the payment due date in respect of the payment, and

        (ii)   the basis on which that sum is calculated.

(3)   A notice complies with this subsection if it specifies—

    (a)   the sum that the payee considers to be or to have been due at the payment due date in respect of the payment, and

    (b)   the basis on which that sum is calculated.

(4)   For the purposes of this section, it is immaterial that the sum referred to in subsection (2)(a) or (b) or (3)(a) may be zero.

(5)   If or to the extent that a contract does not comply with subsection (1), the relevant provisions of the Scheme for Construction Contracts apply.

(6)   In this and the following sections, in relation to any payment provided for by a construction contract—

"payee" means the person to whom the payment is due;
"payer" means the person from whom the payment is due;
"payment due date" means the date provided for by the contract as the date on which the payment is due;
"specified person" means a person specified in or determined in accordance with the provisions of the contract.

110B Payment notices: payee's notice in default of payer's notice

(1)   This section applies in a case where, in relation to any payment provided for by a construction contract—

(a)   the contract requires the payer or a specified person to give the payee a notice complying with section 110A(2) not later than five days after the payment due date, but

(b)   notice is not given as so required.

(2)   Subject to subsection (4), the payee may give to the payer a notice complying with section 110A(3) at any time after the date on which the notice referred to in subsection (1)(a) was required by the contract to be given.

(3)   Where pursuant to subsection (2) the payee gives a notice complying with section 110A(3), the final date for payment of the sum specified in the notice shall for all purposes be regarded as postponed by the same number of days as the number of days after the date referred to in subsection (2) that the notice was given.

(4)   If—

(a)   the contract permits or requires the payee, before the date on which the notice referred to in subsection (1)(a) is required by the contract to be given, to notify the payer or a specified person of—

(i)   the sum that the payee considers will become due on the payment due date in respect of the payment, and

(ii)   the basis on which that sum is calculated, and

(b)   the payee gives such notification in accordance with the contract,

that notification is to be regarded as a notice complying with section 110A(3) given pursuant to subsection (2) (and the payee may not give another such notice pursuant to that subsection).

111   Requirement to pay notified sum

(1)   Subject as follows, where a payment is provided for by a construction contract, the payer must pay the notified sum (to the extent not already paid) on or before the final date for payment.

(2)   For the purposes of this section, the "notified sum" in relation to any payment provided for by a construction contract means—

(a)   in a case where a notice complying with section 110A(2) has been given pursuant to and in accordance with a requirement of the contract, the amount specified in that notice;

(b)   in a case where a notice complying with section 110A(3) has been given pursuant to and in accordance with a requirement of the contract, the amount specified in that notice;

(c)   in a case where a notice complying with section 110A(3) has been given pursuant to and in accordance with section 110B(2), the amount specified in that notice.

(3)   The payer or a specified person may in accordance with this section give to the payee a notice of the payer's intention to pay less than the notified sum.

(4)   A notice under subsection (3) must specify—

(a)   the sum that the payer considers to be due on the date the notice is served, and

(b)   the basis on which that sum is calculated.

It is immaterial for the purposes of this subsection that the sum referred to in paragraph (a) or (b) may be zero.

(5)   A notice under subsection (3)—

(a)   must be given not later than the prescribed period before the final date for payment, and

(b)   in a case referred to in subsection (2)(b) or (c), may not be given before the notice by reference to which the notified sum is determined.

(6)   Where a notice is given under subsection (3), subsection (1) applies only in respect of the sum specified pursuant to subsection (4)(a).

(7)   In subsection (5), "prescribed period" means—

(a)   such period as the parties may agree, or

(b)   in the absence of such agreement, the period provided by the Scheme for Construction Contracts.

(8) Subsection (9) applies where in respect of a payment—
   (a) a notice complying with section 110A(2) has been given pursuant to and in accordance with a requirement of the contract (and no notice under subsection (3) is given), or
   (b) a notice under subsection (3) is given in accordance with this section,
   but on the matter being referred to adjudication the adjudicator decides that more than the sum specified in the notice should be paid.

(9) In a case where this subsection applies, the decision of the adjudicator referred to in subsection (8) shall be construed as requiring payment of the additional amount not later than—
   (a) seven days from the date of the decision, or
   (b) the date which apart from the notice would have been the final date for payment,
   whichever is the later.

(10) Subsection (1) does not apply in relation to a payment provided for by a construction contract where—
   (a) the contract provides that, if the payee becomes insolvent the payer need not pay any sum due in respect of the payment, and
   (b) the payee has become insolvent after the prescribed period referred to in subsection (5)(a).

(11) Subsections (2) to (5) of section 113 apply for the purposes of subsection (10) of this section as they apply for the purposes of that section.

112 Right to suspend performance for non-payment

(1) Where the requirement in section 111(1) applies in relation to any sum but is not complied with, the person to whom the sum is due has the right (without prejudice to any other right or remedy) to suspend performance of any or all of his obligations under the contract to the party by whom payment ought to have been made ("the party in default").

(2) The right may not be exercised without first giving to the party in default at least seven days' notice of intention to suspend performance, stating the ground or grounds on which it is intended to suspend performance.

(3)   The right to suspend performance ceases when the party in default makes payment in full of the sum referred to in subsection (1).

(3A) Where the right conferred by this section is exercised, the party in default shall be liable to pay to the party exercising the right a reasonable amount in respect of costs and expenses reasonably incurred by that party as a result of the exercise of the right.

(4)   Any period during which performance is suspended in pursuance of, or in consequence of the exercise of, the right conferred by this section shall be disregarded in computing for the purposes of any contractual time limit the time taken, by the party exercising the right or by a third party, to complete any work directly or indirectly affected by the exercise of the right.

Where the contractual time limit is set by reference to a date rather than a period, the date shall be adjusted accordingly.

113   Prohibition of conditional payment provisions

(1)   A provision making payment under a construction contract conditional on the payer receiving payment from a third person is ineffective, unless that third person, or any other person payment by whom is under the contract (directly or indirectly) a condition of payment by that third person, is insolvent.

(2)   For the purposes of this section a company becomes insolvent—
   (a)   when it enters administration within the meaning of Schedule B1 to the Insolvency Act 1986,
   (b)   on the appointment of an administrative receiver or a receiver or manager of its property under Chapter I of Part III of that Act, or the appointment of a receiver under Chapter II of that Part,
   (c)   on the passing of a resolution for voluntary winding-up without a declaration of solvency under section 89 of that Act, or
   (d)   on the making of a winding up order under Part IV or V of that Act.

(3)   For the purposes of this section a partnership becomes insolvent—
   (a)   on the making of a winding-up order against it under any provision of the Insolvency Act 1986 as applied by an order under section 420 of that Act, or

(b)   when sequestration is awarded on the estate of the partnership under section 12 of the Bankruptcy (Scotland) Act 1985 or the partnership grants a trust deed for its creditors.

(4)   For the purposes of this section an individual becomes insolvent—

(a)   on the making of a bankruptcy order against him under Part IX of the Insolvency Act 1986, or

(b)   on the sequestration of his estate under the Bankruptcy (Scotland) Act 1985 or when he grants a trust deed for his creditors.

(5)   A company, partnership or individual shall also be treated as insolvent on the occurrence of any event corresponding to those specified in subsection (2), (3) or (4) under the law of Northern Ireland or of a country outside the United Kingdom.

(6)   Where a provision is rendered ineffective by subsection (1), the parties are free to agree other terms for payment.

In the absence of such agreement, the relevant provisions of the Scheme for Construction Contracts apply.

Supplementary provisions

114   The Scheme for Construction Contracts

(1)   The Minister shall by regulations make a scheme ("the Scheme for Construction Contracts") containing provision about the matters referred to in the preceding provisions of this Part.

(2)   Before making any regulations under this section the Minister shall consult such persons as he thinks fit.

(3)   In this section "the Minister" means—

(a)   for England and Wales, the Secretary of State, and

(b)   for Scotland, the Lord Advocate.

(4)   Where any provisions of the Scheme for Construction Contracts apply by virtue of this Part in default of contractual provision agreed by the parties, they have effect as implied terms of the contract concerned.

(5)   Regulations under this section shall not be made unless a draft of them has been approved by resolution of each House of Parliament.

115   Service of notices, etc.

(1)   The parties are free to agree on the manner of service of any notice or other document required or authorised to be served in pursuance of the construction contract or for any of the purposes of this Part.

(2)   If or to the extent that there is no such agreement the following provisions apply.

(3)   A notice or other document may be served on a person by any effective means.

(4)   If a notice or other document is addressed, pre-paid and delivered by post—

   (a)   to the addressee's last known principal residence or, if he is or has been carrying on a trade, profession or business, his last known principal business address, or

   (b)   where the addressee is a body corporate, to the body's registered or principal office,

   it shall be treated as effectively served.

(5)   This section does not apply to the service of documents for the purposes of legal proceedings, for which provision is made by rules of court.

(6)   References in this Part to a notice or other document include any form of communication in writing and references to service shall be construed accordingly.

116   Reckoning periods of time

(1)   For the purposes of this Part periods of time shall be reckoned as follows.

(2)   Where an act is required to be done within a specified period after or from a specified date, the period begins immediately after that date.

(3)   Where the period would include Christmas Day, Good Friday or a day which under the Banking and Financial Dealings Act 1971 is a bank holiday in England and Wales or, as the case may be, in Scotland, that day shall be excluded.

117   Crown application

(1)   This Part applies to a construction contract entered into by or on behalf of the Crown otherwise than by or on behalf of Her Majesty in her private capacity.

(2)   This Part applies to a construction contract entered into on behalf of the Duchy of Cornwall notwithstanding any Crown interest.

(3)   Where a construction contract is entered into by or on behalf of Her Majesty in right of the Duchy of Lancaster, Her Majesty shall be represented, for the purposes of any adjudication or other proceedings

arising out of the contract by virtue of this Part, by the Chancellor of the Duchy or such person as he may appoint.

(4)   Where a construction contract is entered into on behalf of the Duchy of Cornwall, the Duke of Cornwall or the possessor for the time being of the Duchy shall be represented, for the purposes of any adjudication or other proceedings arising out of the contract by virtue of this Part, by such person as he may appoint.

Appendix 2
The Scheme for Construction Contracts

The Scheme for Construction Contracts (England and Wales) Regulations 1998 was partly amended in England, Wales and Scotland to reflect changes made to the Housing Grants, Construction and Regeneration Act 1996 by the Local Democracy, Economic Development and Construction Act 2009. The effect of both the English and Welsh versions was that the 1998 Scheme was amended in a similar way. The amendments were:

- in England – the Scheme for Construction Contracts (England and Wales) Regulations 1998 (Amendment) (England) Regulations 2011, which came into force on 1 October 2011
- in Wales – the Scheme for Construction Contracts (England and Wales) Regulations 1998 (Amendment) (Wales) Regulations 2011 (Scheme for Construction Contracts (Wales) Regulations 2011), which came into force on 1 October 2011
- in Scotland – the Scheme for Construction Contracts (Scotland) Amendment Regulations 2011 (Scheme for Construction Contracts (Scotland) Regulations 2011), which came into force on 1 November 2011.

In Northern Ireland, changes have been brought about by the Construction Contracts (Amendment) Act (Northern Ireland) 2011.

Amendments made to the Scheme by the Scheme for Construction Contracts etc. (England) Regulations 2011 do not apply to construction contracts for construction operations in Wales, Scotland or Northern Ireland. Each set of amendment regulations (or Act in the case of Northern Ireland) applies only to its own part of the UK and may differ slightly from that which is in operation elsewhere. For example, the Scottish amendments require more detail to be given in a payer's payment notice than is required in either the English or Welsh amendments.

It is important to check that if a Scheme for Construction Contracts is to be used in an adjudication then the amendment regulations are the correct ones for that particular part of the UK. It is equally important to check the date of the construction contract because the amended schemes and Act only affect construction contracts which have been entered into after the changes came into force, which was 1 October 2011 for England and Wales, and 1 November 2011 for Scotland.

What are the changes to the Scheme?

Where the parties to a construction contract fail to make provision in their contract for one or more of various terms relating to adjudication, the provisions of Part 1 of the Schedule to the Scheme have effect as implied terms of the parties' contract. The changes to the Scheme in England (which are similar to those in Wales) are:

• upon a dispute being referred to an adjudicator, Regulation 3(3) requires the adjudicator to inform the parties to the contract of the date of the referral
• broadly similar provisions relating to the fees and expenses of an adjudicator are amended by Regulation 3(4), (5) and (13) – the effect of these amendments is to ensure that the adjudicator's ability to look to both parties to the construction contract for the payment of the adjudicator's fees and expenses is subject to any valid, express, contractual provision to the contrary
• Regulation 3(7) amends paragraph 19(1) of the Scheme to make it clear that the period within which an adjudicator must reach a decision begins when the adjudicator receives the Referral Notice
• adjudicators have the power, under Regulation 3(10), to correct (in various circumstances) minor errors in their decisions within five days of the decision
• Regulation 3(11) and (12) repeal provisions allowing for peremptory decisions by adjudicators
• Regulation 4 amends Part 2 of the Schedule to the Scheme which deals with payments. It implies into the contract provisions relating to payments if express terms are absent or deficient
• section 110A of the 1996 Act (as amended) provides that a construction contract must contain a provision to the effect that a *payment notice* (setting out, in relation to every payment, the sum considered due) must be given by the person whom the parties have agreed (i.e. the payer, the payee or certain other persons); where the parties have failed to make express provision in their

contract as to who is to give such notices, Regulation 4(3) substitutes a new paragraph 9 of Part 2 of the Schedule to the Scheme with the effect that this is the payer's responsibility.

• section 111 of the 1996 Act (as amended) introduces a requirement to pay the sum set out in a *payment notice* (whether given pursuant to express terms in the parties' contract or by virtue of new paragraph 9 of Part 2 of the Schedule to the Scheme). It also makes provision for the sum in such a notice to be challenged or revised by the giving of a type of counter-notice, that is, a notice of intention to pay less than the notified sum. Regulation 4(4) substitutes a new paragraph 10 of Part 2 of the Schedule to make provision for the timing of such a counter-notice where the parties have failed to agree on this.

The Scheme for Construction Contracts (England and Wales) Regulations 1998 (Amendment) (England) Regulations 2011

SCHEME FOR CONSTRUCTION CONTRACTS

PART I ADJUDICATION

Notice of Intention to seek Adjudication

1.—(1) Any party to a construction contract (the "referring party") may give written notice (the "notice of adjudication") at any time of his intention to refer any dispute arising under the contract, to adjudication.

(2) The notice of adjudication shall be given to every other party to the contract.

(3) The notice of adjudication shall set out briefly—

(a) the nature and a brief description of the dispute and of the parties involved,

(b) details of where and when the dispute has arisen,

(c) the nature of the redress which is sought, and

(d) the names and addresses of the parties to the contract (including, where appropriate, the addresses which the parties have specified for the giving of notices).

2.—(1) Following the giving of a notice of adjudication and subject to any agreement between the parties to the dispute as to who shall act as adjudicator—

(a) the referring party shall request the person (if any) specified in the contract to act as adjudicator, or

   (b) if no person is named in the contract or the person named has already
        indicated that he is unwilling or unable to act, and the contract
        provides for a specified nominating body to select a person, the refer-
        ring party shall request the nominating body named in the contract to
        select a person to act as adjudicator, or
   (c) where neither paragraph (a) nor (b) above applies, or where the person
        referred to in (a) has already indicated that he is unwilling or unable to act
        and (b) does not apply, the referring party shall request an adjudicator
        nominating body to select a person to act as adjudicator.

(2) A person requested to act as adjudicator in accordance with the provisions
of paragraph (1) shall indicate whether or not he is willing to act within two days
of receiving the request.

(3) In this paragraph, and in paragraphs 5 and 6 below, an "adjudicator nominating body" shall mean a body (not being a natural person and not being a
party to the dispute) which holds itself out publicly as a body which will select an
adjudicator when requested to do so by a referring party.

3. The request referred to in paragraphs 2, 5 and 6 shall be accompanied by a
copy of the notice of adjudication.

4. Any person requested or selected to act as adjudicator in accordance with
paragraphs 2, 5 or 6 shall be a natural person acting in his personal capacity. A
person requested or selected to act as an adjudicator shall not be an employee
of any of the parties to the dispute and shall declare any interest, financial or
otherwise, in any matter relating to the dispute.

5.—(1) The nominating body referred to in paragraphs 2(1)(b) and 6(1)(b) or
the adjudicator nominating body referred to in paragraphs 2(1)(c), 5(2)(b) and
6(1)(c) must communicate the selection of an adjudicator to the referring party
within five days of receiving a request to do so.

(2) Where the nominating body or the adjudicator nominating body fails to
comply with paragraph (1), the referring party may—
   (a) agree with the other party to the dispute to request a specified person
        to act as adjudicator, or
   (b) request any other adjudicator nominating body to select a person to
        act as adjudicator.

(3) The person requested to act as adjudicator in accordance with the provisions of paragraphs (1) or (2) shall indicate whether or not he is willing to act
within two days of receiving the request.

6.—(1) Where an adjudicator who is named in the contract indicates to the parties that he is unable or unwilling to act, or where he fails to respond in accordance with paragraph 2(2), the referring party may—

(a) request another person (if any) specified in the contract to act as adjudicator, or

(b) request the nominating body (if any) referred to in the contract to select a person to act as adjudicator, or

(c) request any other adjudicator nominating body to select a person to act as adjudicator.

(2) The person requested to act in accordance with the provisions of paragraph (1) shall indicate whether or not he is willing to act within two days of receiving the request.

7.—(1) Where an adjudicator has been selected in accordance with paragraphs 2, 5 or 6, the referring party shall, not later than seven days from the date of the notice of adjudication, refer the dispute in writing (the "referral notice") to the adjudicator.

(2) A referral notice shall be accompanied by copies of, or relevant extracts from, the construction contract and such other documents as the referring party intends to rely upon.

(3) The referring party shall, at the same time as he sends to the adjudicator the documents referred to in paragraphs (1) and (2), send copies of those documents to every other party to the dispute. Upon receipt of the referral notice, the adjudicator must inform every party to the dispute of the date that it was received.

8.—(1) The adjudicator may, with the consent of all the parties to those disputes, adjudicate at the same time on more than one dispute under the same contract.

(2) The adjudicator may, with the consent of all the parties to those disputes, adjudicate at the same time on related disputes under different contracts, whether or not one or more of those parties is a party to those disputes.

(3) All the parties in paragraphs (1) and (2) respectively may agree to extend the period within which the adjudicator may reach a decision in relation to all or any of these disputes.

(4) Where an adjudicator ceases to act because a dispute is to be adjudicated on by another person in terms of this paragraph, that adjudicator's fees and expenses shall be determined in accordance with paragraph 25.

9.—(1) An adjudicator may resign at any time on giving notice in writing to the parties to the dispute.

(2) An adjudicator must resign where the dispute is the same or substantially the same as one which has previously been referred to adjudication, and a decision has been taken in that adjudication.

(3) Where an adjudicator ceases to act under paragraph 9(1)—

    (a) the referring party may serve a fresh notice under paragraph 1 and shall request an adjudicator to act in accordance with paragraphs 2 to 7; and

    (b) if requested by the new adjudicator and insofar as it is reasonably practicable, the parties shall supply him with copies of all documents which they had made available to the previous adjudicator.

(4) Where an adjudicator resigns in the circumstances referred to in paragraph (2), or where a dispute varies significantly from the dispute referred to him in the referral notice and for that reason he is not competent to decide it, the adjudicator shall be entitled to the payment of such reasonable amount as he may determine by way of fees and expenses reasonably incurred by him. Subject to any contractual provision pursuant to section 108A(2) of the Act, the adjudicator may determine how the payment is to be apportioned and the parties are jointly and severally liable for any sum which remains outstanding following the making of any such determination.

10. Where any party to the dispute objects to the appointment of a particular person as adjudicator, that objection shall not invalidate the adjudicator's appointment nor any decision he may reach in accordance with paragraph 20.

11.—(1) The parties to a dispute may at any time agree to revoke the appointment of the adjudicator. The adjudicator shall be entitled to the payment of such reasonable amount as he may determine by way of fees and expenses incurred by him. Subject to any contractual provision pursuant to section 108A(2) of the Act, the adjudicator may determine how the payment is to be apportioned and the parties are jointly and severally liable for any sum which remains outstanding following the making of any such determination.

(2) Where the revocation of the appointment of the adjudicator is due to the default or misconduct of the adjudicator, the parties shall not be liable to pay the adjudicator's fees and expenses.

Powers of the adjudicator

12. The adjudicator shall—

(a) act impartially in carrying out his duties and shall do so in accordance with any relevant terms of the contract and shall reach his decision in accordance with the applicable law in relation to the contract; and

(b) avoid incurring unnecessary expense.

13. The adjudicator may take the initiative in ascertaining the facts and the law necessary to determine the dispute, and shall decide on the procedure to be followed in the adjudication. In particular he may—

(a) request any party to the contract to supply him with such documents as he may reasonably require including, if he so directs, any written statement from any party to the contract supporting or supplementing the referral notice and any other documents given under paragraph 7(2),

(b) decide the language or languages to be used in the adjudication and whether a translation of any document is to be provided and if so by whom,

(c) meet and question any of the parties to the contract and their representatives,

(d) subject to obtaining any necessary consent from a third party or parties, make such site visits and inspections as he considers appropriate, whether accompanied by the parties or not,

(e) subject to obtaining any necessary consent from a third party or parties, carry out any tests or experiments,

(f) obtain and consider such representations and submissions as he requires, and, provided he has notified the parties of his intention, appoint experts, assessors or legal advisers,

(g) give directions as to the timetable for the adjudication, any deadlines, or limits as to the length of written documents or oral representations to be complied with, and

(h) issue other directions relating to the conduct of the adjudication.

14. The parties shall comply with any request or direction of the adjudicator in relation to the adjudication.

15. If, without showing sufficient cause, a party fails to comply with any request, direction or timetable of the adjudicator made in accordance with his powers, fails to produce any document or written statement requested by the adjudicator, or in any other way fails to comply with a requirement under these provisions relating to the adjudication, the adjudicator may—

(a) continue the adjudication in the absence of that party or of the document or written statement requested,

(b) draw such inferences from that failure to comply as the circumstances may, in the adjudicator's opinion, justify, and

(c) make a decision on the basis of the information before him attaching such weight as he thinks fit to any evidence submitted to him outside any period he may have requested or directed.

16.—(1) Subject to any agreement between the parties to the contrary, and to the terms of paragraph (2) below, any party to the dispute may be assisted by, or represented by, such advisers or representatives (whether legally qualified or not) as he considers appropriate.

(2) Where the adjudicator is considering oral evidence or representations, a party to the dispute may not be represented by more than one person, unless the adjudicator gives directions to the contrary.

17. The adjudicator shall consider any relevant information submitted to him by any of the parties to the dispute and shall make available to them any information to be taken into account in reaching his decision.

18. The adjudicator and any party to the dispute shall not disclose to any other person any information or document provided to him in connection with the adjudication which the party supplying it has indicated is to be treated as confidential, except to the extent that it is necessary for the purposes of, or in connection with, the adjudication.

19.—(1) The adjudicator shall reach his decision not later than—

(a) twenty eight days after receipt of the referral notice mentioned in paragraph 7(1), or

(b) forty two days after receipt of the referral notice if the referring party so consents, or

(c) such period exceeding twenty eight days after receipt of the referral notice as the parties to the dispute may, after the giving of that notice, agree.

(2) Where the adjudicator fails, for any reason, to reach his decision in accordance with paragraph (1)

(a) any of the parties to the dispute may serve a fresh notice under paragraph 1 and shall request an adjudicator to act in accordance with paragraphs 2 to 7; and

> (b) if requested by the new adjudicator and insofar as it is reasonably practicable, the parties shall supply him with copies of all documents which they had made available to the previous adjudicator.

(3) As soon as possible after he has reached a decision, the adjudicator shall deliver a copy of that decision to each of the parties to the contract.

Adjudicator's decision

20. The adjudicator shall decide the matters in dispute. He may take into account any other matters which the parties to the dispute agree should be within the scope of the adjudication or which are matters under the contract which he considers are necessarily connected with the dispute. In particular, he may—

> (a) open up, revise and review any decision taken or any certificate given by any person referred to in the contract unless the contract states that the decision or certificate is final and conclusive,
>
> (b) decide that any of the parties to the dispute is liable to make a payment under the contract (whether in sterling or some other currency) and, subject to section 111(9) of the Act, when that payment is due and the final date for payment,
>
> (c) having regard to any term of the contract relating to the payment of interest decide the circumstances in which, and the rates at which, and the periods for which simple or compound rates of interest shall be paid.

21. In the absence of any directions by the adjudicator relating to the time for performance of his decision, the parties shall be required to comply with any decision of the adjudicator immediately on delivery of the decision to the parties.

22. If requested by one of the parties to the dispute, the adjudicator shall provide reasons for his decision.

22A.—(1) The adjudicator may on his own initiative or on the application of a party correct his decision so as to remove a clerical or typographical error arising by accident or omission.

(2) Any correction of a decision must be made within five days of the delivery of the decision to the parties.

(3) As soon as possible after correcting a decision in accordance with this paragraph, the adjudicator must deliver a copy of the corrected decision to each of the parties to the contract.

(4) Any correction of a decision forms part of the decision.

Effects of the decision

23.—(1) [Omitted].

(2) The decision of the adjudicator shall be binding on the parties, and they shall comply with it until the dispute is finally determined by legal proceedings, by arbitration (if the contract provides for arbitration or the parties otherwise agree to arbitration) or by agreement between the parties.

24. [Omitted].

25. The adjudicator shall be entitled to the payment of such reasonable amount as he may determine by way of fees and expenses reasonably incurred by him. Subject to any contractual provision pursuant to section 108A(2) of the Act, the adjudicator may determine how the payment is to be apportioned and the parties are jointly and severally liable for any sum which remains outstanding following the making of any such determination.

26. The adjudicator shall not be liable for anything done or omitted in the discharge or purported discharge of his functions as adjudicator unless the act or omission is in bad faith, and any employee or agent of the adjudicator shall be similarly protected from liability.

PART II PAYMENT

Entitlement to and amount of stage payments

1. Where the parties to a relevant construction contract fail to agree—
  (a) the amount of any instalment or stage or periodic payment for any work under the contract, or
  (b) the intervals at which, or circumstances in which, such payments become due under that contract, or
  (c) both of the matters mentioned in sub-paragraphs (a) and (b) above,
the relevant provisions of paragraphs 2 to 4 below shall apply.

2.—(1) The amount of any payment by way of instalments or stage or periodic payments in respect of a relevant period shall be the difference between the amount determined in accordance with sub-paragraph (2) and the amount determined in accordance with sub-paragraph (3).

(2) The aggregate of the following amounts—
  (a) an amount equal to the value of any work performed in accordance with the relevant construction contract during the period from the commencement of the contract to the end of the relevant period (excluding any amount calculated in accordance with subparagraph (b)),

    (b) where the contract provides for payment for materials, an amount equal to the value of any materials manufactured on site or brought onto site for the purposes of the works during the period from the commencement of the contract to the end of the relevant period, and

    (c) any other amount or sum which the contract specifies shall be payable during or in respect of the period from the commencement of the contract to the end of the relevant period.

(3) The aggregate of any sums which have been paid or are due for payment by way of instalments, stage or periodic payments during the period from the commencement of the contract to the end of the relevant period.

(4) An amount calculated in accordance with this paragraph shall not exceed the difference between—

    (a) the contract price, and

    (b) the aggregate of the instalments or stage or periodic payments which have become due.

Dates for payment

3. Where the parties to a construction contract fail to provide an adequate mechanism for determining either what payments become due under the contract, or when they become due for payment, or both, the relevant provisions of paragraphs 4 to 7 shall apply.

4. Any payment of a kind mentioned in paragraph 2 above shall become due on whichever of the following dates occurs later—

    (a) the expiry of 7 days following the relevant period mentioned in paragraph 2(1) above, or

    (b) the making of a claim by the payee.

5. The final payment payable under a relevant construction contract, namely the payment of an amount equal to the difference (if any) between—

    (a) the contract price, and

    (b) the aggregate of any instalment or stage or periodic payments which have become due under the contract,

shall become due on—

    (a) the expiry of 30 days following completion of the work, or

    (b) the making of a claim by the payee,

whichever is the later.

6. Payment of the contract price under a construction contract (not being a relevant construction contract) shall become due on—

    (a) the expiry of 30 days following the completion of the work, or

    (b) the making of a claim by the payee,

whichever is the later.

7. Any other payment under a construction contract shall become due—

    (a) on the expiry of 7 days following the completion of the work to which the payment relates, or

    (b) the making of a claim by the payee,

whichever is the later.

Final date for payment

8.—(1) Where the parties to a construction contract fail to provide a final date for payment in relation to any sum which becomes due under a construction contract, the provisions of this paragraph shall apply.

(2) The final date for the making of any payment of a kind mentioned in paragraphs 2, 5, 6 or 7, shall be 17 days from the date that payment becomes due.

Payment notice

9.—(1) Where the parties to a construction contract fail, in relation to a payment provided for by the contract, to provide for the issue of a payment notice pursuant to section 110A(1) of the Act, the provisions of this paragraph apply.

(2) The payer must, not later than five days after the payment due date, give a notice to the payee complying with sub-paragraph (3).

(3) A notice complies with this sub-paragraph if it specifies the sum that the payer considers to be due or to have been due at the payment due date and the basis on which that sum is calculated.

(4) For the purposes of this paragraph, it is immaterial that the sum referred to in sub-paragraph (3) may be zero.

(5) A payment provided for by the contract includes any payment of the kind mentioned in paragraph 2, 5, 6, or 7 above.

Notice of intention to pay less than the notified sum

10. Where, in relation to a notice of intention to pay less than the notified sum mentioned in section 111(3) of the Act, the parties fail to agree the prescribed period mentioned in section 111(5), that notice must be given not later than seven days before the final date for payment determined either in accordance with the construction contract, or where no such provision is made in the contract, in accordance with paragraph 8 above.

Prohibition of conditional payment provisions

11. Where a provision making payment under a construction contract conditional on the payer receiving payment from a third person is ineffective as mentioned in section 113 of the Act, and the parties have not agreed other terms for payment, the relevant provisions of—

(a) paragraphs 2, 4, 5, 7, 8, 9 and 10 shall apply in the case of a relevant construction contract, and

(b) paragraphs 6, 7, 8, 9 and 10 shall apply in the case of any other construction contract.

Interpretation

12. In this Part of the Scheme for Construction Contracts—

"claim by the payee" means a written notice given by the party carrying out work under a construction contract to the other party specifying the amount of any payment or payments which he considers to be due and the basis on which it is, or they are calculated;

"contract price" means the entire sum payable under the construction contract in respect of the work;

"relevant construction contract" means any construction contract other than one—

(a) which specifies that the duration of the work is to be less than 45 days, or

(b) in respect of which the parties agree that the duration of the work is estimated to be less than 45 days;

"relevant period" means a period which is specified in, or is calculated by reference to the construction contract or where no such period is so specified or is so calculable, a period of 28 days;

"value of work" means an amount determined in accordance with the construction contract under which the work is performed or where the contract contains no such provision, the cost of any work performed in accordance with that contract together with an amount equal to any overhead or profit included in the contract price;

"work" means any of the work or services mentioned in section 104 of the Act.

Index

Page numbers in italics refer to tables.